W9-BPJ-375

PRICING WITH CONFIDENCE

PRICING WITH CONFIDENCE

10 WAYS TO STOP LEAVING MONEY ON THE TABLE

REED K. HOLDEN
MARK R. BURTON

WILEY

John Wiley & Sons, Inc.

Published by John Wiley & Sons, Inc., Hoboken, New Jersey.
Published simultaneously in Canada.

For general information on our other products and services please contact our Customer Care
Department within the U.S. at (800) 762-2974, outside the United States at (317) 572-3993 or fax
(317) 572-4002.

Wiley also publishes its books in a variety of electronic formats. Some content that appears in print
may not be available in electronic books. For more information about Wiley products, visit our web
site at www.wiley.com.

Library of Congress Cataloging-in-Publication Data:

Reed K. Holden, Mark. R. Burton
  Pricing with confidence : 10 ways to stop leaving money on the table/
Reed K. Holden, Mark R. Burton.
    p. cm.
  ISBN 978-0-470-19757-8 (cloth)
  1. Pricing.   2. Service industries—Prices.   I. Burton, Mark, 1965–   II. Title.
  HF5416.5.H647 2008
  658.8'16—dc22   2007033362

Printed in the United States of America.

10   9   8   7   6   5   4

Dedicated to:

Carolyn Holden
Co-Founder and President

Who made this book a reality

and

John A. Burton

Wish you could be here

The essence of strategy is the efficient allocation of scarce resources so as to maximize their return to the organization.

—David C.D. Rogers

CONTENTS

ACKNOWLEDGMENTS

Books like this don't just spring out of the authors' collective wisdom; they come from what is learned in interactions with a wide range of professionals over the years. These are the people in the arena who have learned good pricing practices through experience. While it's impossible to name everyone, we'd like to thank some special people who have provided an incredible amount of support and insight.

When we started Holden Advisors, we did exploratory work on our new Value Discipline model with a number of pricing, marketing, and sales managers who provided terrific insights for the start of this work: Lewie Miller of Sant Corp., who is also on our board of advisors; Chris Hylen, now of Intuit; Scott Zimmerman of GE Medical; Greg Reid of Yellow-Roadway; Michael Bogosian; Ray Sharpe of Isola; Dan Thornton, now of RR Donnelley; Alan Yamamoto of IBM; Mary McMahon of Unisys; our good friend David Philips of Vulcan Materials, who also advised on this book; Debra Meredith of Cardinal Presource; Alan Hollander, now of Avaya; Brian Weinstein of Monster Worldwide; Joe Marigliano, now of American Standard; Joe Megan of Metavante; Josh Rossman, now of Microsoft; Navdeep Sodhi of Kennametal; Frank Connoly of Harris Interactive; Joe Panaro of MasterCard International; and Andy Slusher of Yellow-Roadway, who was also an advisor on book content; and, importantly, Eric Mitchell and the team at Professional Pricing Society.

As the book began to develop, we relied on a kitchen cabinet of external advisors to help us shape title, primary content, and graphics. These people did great work in providing valuable insights quickly so we could meet our deadlines. While all content and recollections are ours and correct to the best of our knowledge, we'd like to thank the following for their insights and support: Dirk Meyer, and Marty Seyer of AMD; Henri Richard of Freescale. David Philips of Vulcan Materials; Ron Baker of The Verasage Institute; Denise Hansard of Thermo-Fisher Scientific; Adele McLean of ICan Solutions; Jim Geisman of MarketShare Inc.; Dan Nimer; Sam Wee of SAP; David Sugano of Schering Plough; Tom Snead; Mike Twamley of Standard & Poor's; John Sleeting of General Electric; Brent Melancon of Medtronic CardioVascular; Andy Slusher of YRWC; Lydia Zownirenko Kersey of Pass & Seymour; Lewie Miller of Sant Corp.; Mike Allen, who also serves on our Board of Advisors; Gene Zelek of Freeborn & Peters, who also serves on our Board of Advisors; Andy Stotler of BASF; Bob Cross of Revenue Analytics; Judith Weiss; and Laura Ramos of Forrester Research.

We couldn't have done this project without the ongoing support of our colleagues at Holden Advisors. This includes Nelson Hyde, Ann Marie Trebendis, Steve Haggett, and our Co-Founder and President, Carolyn Holden.

We'd also like to thank those who have moved on to different pastures yet helped in the early research for the model insights for the book: Rachel Jacobson, Mike Lawson, Susanna Barmakian, Curtis Bingham, Andrew Namiot, and Ellen Quackenbush. We'd also like to acknowledge the good work of Andrew Holden from the University of Massachusetts and Professor Richard Hanna of Boston College.

The core book team was made up of a number of dedicated and talented individuals headed up by Carolyn Holden to whom this book is in part dedicated. John Kador is our internal editor who provided terrific help in converting our pricing-speak into language for nonpricing professionals. John has been a great partner and facilitator of our writing process and he has become a respected friend. Tom Sant of Sant Corp. and Hyde Park Partners gave us an early critique on writing styles that helped shape our new directions. Our editor at Wiley, Richard Narramore, who, along with Tiffany Groglio, provided valuable insights for the positioning of the content. Kim Railsback did great work on the book cover and allegedly used one of the authors for a model. Victoria Webber of Graphware provided tremendous feedback and helped with all of the book's internal graphics.

INTRODUCTION

Why Pricing Is So Hard and Why Most Companies Mess It Up

You're the Salesperson

Imagine you are a salesperson trying to sell a product for $10,000. The customer's purchasing agent responds that a competing supplier is selling a similar product for $8,000.

What would you do?

Let's look at your options. If you have pricing authority, you can choose to match the price of the lower offer. If you can't control price, you go back to your manager or pricing department and ask them for the authority to match the competitor's price. If you get it, maybe you'll be lucky: The customer will sign with you for $8,000, and you'll earn your commission. But most salespeople in this situation know the outcome will be different.

Salespeople know the situation will typically play out as follows: The purchasing agent won't be content with a $2,000 discount. The buyer will go back to the losing supplier and get them to lower their price even further, starting a back-and-forth process that we call the *pricing death spiral*. This process, where smart buyers try to squeeze every last penny out of their vendors, is good only for the buyers. With a pricing death spiral, there are no winners. Only survivors.

Pricing with confidence—the subject of this book—allows you to avoid the pricing death spiral. The approach outlined in this book will help you close the deal without leaving discount dollars on the table. The approach is not difficult, but it requires preparation; a detailed knowledge of your offering, your competitors' offering, and the competitive landscape; as well as a deep awareness of the customer's real objectives and requirements.

With pricing confidence, when the purchasing agent mentions the bid from one of your competitors, your response will be different. "The throughput of the competing machine is half of ours," you will say to the purchasing agent. "Your engineers told us they needed the throughput of our product to increase your product yield. But if you don't think the throughput of our product is really required, we're pleased to offer you a machine that gives you 60 percent of the throughput for $7,900. Which do you prefer?"

Now the purchasing agent is on the defensive. If the purchasing agent insists on a lower price, he can get it but will have to accept a lower-value product. If, as is more likely the case, the increased throughput is essential, the purchasing agent must acknowledge that fact and be prepared to pay the higher price that reflects the increased value your product delivers. Whether the customer buys the lower-value product (whose price beats the competition) or the higher-value product (whose performance beats the competition), you come out ahead. That's confidence in pricing, and that's what this book is all about.

10 Rules of Engagement

Pricing with confidence requires an understanding of 10 rules of engagement. Each rule is a general reminder to all members of the firm of what is needed to grow both profits and revenue in increasingly competitive and price-oriented markets. Here, in brief, are the 10 rules to pricing confidence.

Rule One: Replace the Discounting Habit with a Little Arrogance

The best way to dislodge any deep-rooted habit is to replace it with another.

Price discounting is entrenched in most organizations. As with any addiction, the discounting habit is tough to break cold turkey. The best way to dislodge any deep-rooted attitude is to replace it with another. Arrogance, feeling good about your products and services, provides the confidence needed to kick the discounting habit. Simple analysis can point to where bad discounting leaves money on the table.

Rule Two: Understand the Value You Offer to Your Customer

How can customers be expected to understand your value if you don't?

You can't have confidence in your pricing until you have confidence in the financial value that your offerings create for customers. Even though many managers are convinced they can't get this information, the reality is that most of your customers are eager to tell you. All it takes is asking the right questions and being willing to listen.

Rule Three: Apply One of Three Simple Pricing Strategies

When to price high, when to price low, and a strategy for everything in between.

Strategies can and should be simple and agreed to by everyone in the firm. Without this, you can't have confidence in your prices.

Rule Four: Play Better Poker with Customers

Learn to love your price buyers but play better poker with your poker players.

Most customers say that value is what they most want, but many are bluffing when they ask for a discount. Some customers are motivated by price alone. Others want—and are willing to pay for—value. It's the poker players you've got to control. Adjust your offering and selling approach to optimize your advantage for each. Know the difference, so the difference can work for you. You might even learn to love your price buyers.

Rule Five: Price to Increase Profits

The only effective thing that better pricing should accomplish for companies is to increase profits.

It's a myth that if you discount price to increase sales, you will see increased profits. Profits result when an organization does many things right, including pricing. Efficiency, controlling costs, better profit metrics—all are required for pricing success.

Rule Six: Add New Products and Services that Give You Negotiating Flexibility and Growth

When your products are regarded as commodities, add services to differentiate products and prop up prices.

Provide your salespeople with the gives and gets that are so important in negotiating. When products are regarded as commodities, add services to differentiate products and prop up prices. This strategy is undermined when valuable services are given away. To gain more confidence in negotiating, you can price incremental services to reflect their true value to customers. An effective strategy for market dominance is to develop a dual offering that covers both the high- and low-end customer needs. Flanking offerings grow both the revenue and the global footprint of the firm. If customers want a lower price, subtract features and services.

Rule Seven: Force Your Competitor to React to Your Pricing

Smart players know they don't have to participate in a competitive pricing death spiral.

Every player enjoys one or more value advantages. The trick is to use your value to stop leaving money on the table. Smart players know they don't have to participate in a competitive pricing death spiral. They map their markets. They define where they do and do not have a value advantage over their competitors. They know where and how to compete on price. Most important, they know where and how not to.

Rule Eight: Build Your Selling Backbone

The best pricing strategy will fail unless salespeople and managers have backbone in the selling process and the ability to defend it.

Confidence in negotiation requires confidence in pricing. Confidence in pricing comes from knowing the value of your products or services. It also comes from knowing your customer. Backbone comes from knowing the tricks your customers use to get you to drop price and how to deal with them.

Rule Nine: Take Simple Steps to Move from Cost-Plus to Value-Based Pricing

There is nothing wrong with cost-plus pricing as long as it does a good job of leveraging the financial value you create for customers.

Value-based pricing is an ideal. It requires sophisticated internal skills and systems. The trick to value-based pricing is to evolve pricing as the discipline and skills of your people improve. Start gradually. There is nothing wrong with cost-plus pricing as long as it does a good job of leveraging the financial value you create for customers. Once you learn those skills, moving forward to real value-based pricing is a snap.

Rule Ten: Price with Confidence: Remember Who You Are

Shift the negotiation to how you provide concrete results for your customers.

Customers buy results, not rhetoric. Moving beyond the rhetoric of value will enable you to prove those results to customers. By applying these 10 actionable rules, you can have confidence in your pricing decisions. You can move the negotiation to a discussion of how you provide concrete results for your customers. Your firm will earn more profits and revenue by capturing the money you're currently leaving on the table.

What Is Your Pricing Purpose?

What are you trying to accomplish when you set prices?

Sure, it seems like a simple question. Business 101 tells us that price is one of the four major elements of the marketing mix. Price is one of the Four Ps, the others being Product, Promotion, and Place. Business 101 tells us that the right price should meet the requirement of the buyer and seller. If you hit the optimum price, the theory suggests, your customers will be happier, your profits will be higher, and your bottom line will be healthier.

In reality, pricing is far from simple. Setting the optimum price is one of the most difficult decisions managers ever make. Most companies are so bad at it that they leave money on the table. Lots of it. This book will help you optimize the pricing of your business-to-business products and services so that the money goes in your pocket.

Pricing is about more than setting prices. Pricing represents a strategy to increase sales volume at a profit while incorporating and communicating critical messages about the value the offering delivers to the customer. In general, most organizations fail to use pricing in such a disciplined fashion. Something else happens, of course, but many organizations don't figure this out until it's too late.

There are four pricing strategies that organizations typically employ. Let's take a look at each of these.

1. *Price to Cover Costs:* Here, you set prices based on your costs and add a reasonable margin. It makes sense to do this because if you always price to provide a profit over your costs, you'll make money. Right? Not necessarily. There are two problems with Price to Cover Costs. First, your customers don't care about your costs. They care only about the value you deliver. By ignoring the value that you create for customers, cost-based pricing can keep prices lower than they should be, thus leaving money on the table and reducing profits. On the flip side, pricing to cover costs can actually keep prices higher than optimum, thus reducing sales. The second problem with cost-based pricing is that it allocates overhead and/or fixed plant costs into pricing calculations. Sounds reasonable until you consider that often those costs appear to be variable when they aren't. If you have low utilizations, your allocations are going to be high, preventing you from dropping the price to increase sales and subsequently the utilization. Again, you either forfeit profits or sales. Sometimes both.

2. *Pricing to Meet the Market:* If you know that your costing systems inflate the true costs, maybe you use market-based pricing. Here, organizations let the market set the price. We hear about this strategy a lot and on the surface it sounds good. After all, we know that the market alone sets prices. Here's the problem with Pricing to Meet the Market: We don't sell to markets. We sell to customers. And customers, being unique, often surprise us by behaving differently than markets predict they will. They ask for a lower price, and we give it to them. In the end, market-based pricing is just lowering price to close a deal.

3. *Pricing to Close a Deal:* Now we're on to something. Pricing to close a deal is what business and pricing should be all about. After all, if we can't price to close a deal, what good is pricing? The process should work to provide us with a profit, right? Well, not really. When you price to close a deal, it provides customers with every incentive to negotiate for lower prices. These customers put salespeople through a meat grinder of price negotiations. The process, in turn, gives salespeople every incentive to respond with lower prices. It undermines their confidence in prices and leaves money on the table.

4. *Pricing to Gain Market Share:* In this strategy, prices are set low to gain share against a competitor. Again, this sounds like a good idea. We all learned that increasing market share leads to increases in profits. The reality is not that clear-cut. If you already enjoy high market share, it's true you're going to be more profitable. But, it's more likely that you are not the market share leader. In that case, using lower prices to go after market share is risky. You can't expect to catch your competitors by surprise. Even if you do, the advantage will be temporary. Most likely, the market leader will simply match your price. Lower prices eat into profits of both companies. Customers love a price war.

The problem is that these strategies are often in place at the same company. Often, each department uses a different strategy. And, those strategies are not only in conflict with each other but they also fail to effectively provide profitable sales. Instead, they can undermine revenue and profits.

Yes, but We Need to Meet the Numbers

As business managers, we learn to set financial objectives and then drive the people in the business to meet those numbers. That's what our bosses expect. That's what the analysts expect. There are a number of problems associated with driving employees to meet financial or other objectives, especially if meeting short-term goals is allowed to eclipse long-term objectives. But that's the subject for another book.

This is a book on pricing, so let's look at the problems of using price to meet specific objectives. In almost all cases, we are talking about applying price discounts to meet short-term sales objectives. Unfortunately, the results of this strategy are almost always unsatisfactory. It's not hard to see why. Discounting simply trains customers to hold off placing their orders in anticipation of even deeper discounts. But there's a bigger problem than leaving money on the table. Rather than selling your products and services because customers derive value from them, you end up selling them just to meet your numbers. It's never sustainable to exchange short-term opportunism for long-term customer development. You may get a high from the adrenalin rush of the end-of-quarter madness, but you end up leaving so much money on the table, you might get asked to leave the game.

It's a game that almost all businesses play. Every year, managers make projections—a fancy name for setting goals—for the organization to meet. And by managers, we include everyone from the executive suite to team leaders and project managers. These projections get reported down the chain of command, workers get their marching orders, and everyone waits for the results to be reported up the chain of command. If it turns out that the company has hit its projections, satisfaction abounds. It's a sign that management understands the market and is in control of the business. It's considered satisfactory if the company outperforms the projections. It's taken as evidence of particularly talented managers. No one asks why the particularly talented managers missed their projections by setting the targets too low.

Cycles of Desperation

What happens if the results start coming up short of projections? Let's back up a step. When goals are set for the corporation, they trickle down to the divisions, business units, and regions. These projections are based on guesswork. Managers prefer the term *assumptions.* The assumptions take the form of forward-looking estimates about interest rates, prices of raw materials, energy costs, manufacturing capacity, and distribution logistics. The assumptions also factor in the likely behavior of competitors. All these numbers are crunched, and the resulting spreadsheets are quite impressive. But managers can't have much confidence in assumptions driven by variables that are, by definition, uncontrollable and unpredictable. Then the managers consider the one resource that they can control: their sales force. Many business forecasts are driven by assumptions about the sales force's ability to deliver the numbers the managers promise. There are two critical problems with this reality. First, most managers typically overestimate their ability to get salespeople to deliver specific outcomes. But, the second problem is even more destructive. The business loses sight of what should be its main goal: delivering long-term value for its customers. Instead, its focus shifts to meeting numbers to keep managers and investors happy.

Take a look at the situation from the point of view of the sales force. When salespeople get their objectives for the year, they base their ability to deliver results on a number of assumptions of their own. Assumptions such as having the right product mix, delivering products on time, and getting a feel for what competitors do. This is where the wheels begin to fall off the wagon. Nothing ever happens as projected. Interest rates go up. Currency exchange becomes unfavorable. Product delivery is interrupted. Competitors drop prices (imagine that). Customers *seem* to get more price-sensitive. When things don't go as expected, it leads to what we call *cycles of desperation.*

Suppose that the salespeople have been trained to negotiate well. Or perhaps they have a limit to what price they can drop to. In either case, the results are the same. Salespeople do the best they can to hold the line. Do they get rewarded for that? Nope. What happens is that at the end of the period—month, quarter, or year—the organization is short of the projections. Managers finally get off their collective behinds and go out to do what is necessary to close the gap. That means closing business with customers, whatever it takes. There's an old business adage that says that if the only tool you have is a hammer, all problems look like nails. So it is with managers who need to make the numbers. They have a problem, and the only tool they have is price.

The White Horse Syndrome

We call it the White Horse Syndrome in honor of television shows in which a complicated problem of long duration is resolved when a hero such as the Lone Ranger rides into town in a cloud of dust on a white horse to save the day. Then, as quickly as he arrives, the hero departs, saving everyone the unpleasant task of asking awkward questions such as "How did we get into this mess?" Today's managers also want to be regarded as heroes, saving the day, avoiding awkward questions. Instead what they usually do is drop prices. And in so doing, they shoot themselves and their company in the foot.

This is because customers learn to focus their negotiations on discounts. When we are in the market for a new car, most of us have learned to shop on the last day of the month, when salespeople, desperate to make their sales quotas for the month, are most willing to discount.

We know of one manager who refused to play this no-win game until the division president got desperate. It was a business downturn, and his bonus was at risk if the company did not deliver the numbers. The executive's reaction was predictable. He authorized an end-of-month discount to distributors who would buy forward. The results in the first month were great: The company made its numbers that month.

The next month was different, of course. Customers had placed that month's order the prior month to obtain the generous discount. What did the executive do? This time he offered another discount for buyers who would buy before the end of the month. Did the company make its numbers? No. Remember, they were in a business downturn. The company needed to adjust its expectations, not use price to make unreasonable numbers.

The company stopped its lunacy in the third month and decided to face the music. In the last week of the third month, the distributors were clearly holding their orders, waiting for another price cut. When the additional price cuts didn't materialize, customers started calling, asking when the discounts would be coming. When they heard that there were no more discounts, they started placing their orders as they had done in the past. Using price as the primary competitive weapon in most markets doesn't buy any additional business; it just gets customers to focus more on price and less on value. The executive missed his numbers and had to forfeit his bonus. But worse, the company lost hundreds of thousands of dollars in profits by offering discounts they didn't have to.

How about the effect of the White Horse Syndrome on the sales force? The salespeople quickly learn that if the managers are going to focus on price, they should, too. As a consequence, they stop focusing on value. They worry less about being good negotiators. When a customer asks for a lower price, they either give it to them or say they have to check with their manager. In either case, the customer knows they have won. Salespeople begin to have less regard for what is in the long-term interests of the company. They stop listening to the value rhetoric coming out of senior executives' mouths.

To make matters worse, the firms that buy into the White Horse Syndrome begin to develop systems that formalize the dysfunctional process. Forms and policies are created to dictate who can control price. Whole departments spring up to support the process. Price exception requests accumulate. Everyone learns how to play the game. Smart salespeople learn how to be the squeaky wheel that demands and obtains the lower price for their customers. Uncontrollable discounting becomes part of the corporate culture, embedded in the corporate DNA, unexamined and unexaminable. Confidence in any pricing strategy goes out the window.

Then the gross rationalization starts. Executives start feeling sorry for themselves, mistaking the difficult conditions they have created for a state of affairs they cannot control. The mantra becomes "Boy, it's a brutal industry we're in." Pessimism becomes almost a badge of honor. Talk about value is dismissed as irrelevant. "Hah! Value selling will never work in our industry. It's too tough here," they say. Fortunately, nothing could be further from the truth.

A Fool's Game

Price competition is a fool's game. How many times have you agreed to a low price because a competitor was doing it? We all have. You want to beat the competitor at their own game. After all, if they can discount, you can do discount better. We all know what happens then. If you lose the order, you get mad because you were undercut. But, if you do win the order, your satisfaction is quickly undermined by the sneaking suspicion that what you have won is a Pyrrhic victory (another such victory and we are done for!). When you are away from the heat of battle and can consult the costing sheets, you determine that you've actually lost money on the order. That's okay, you tell yourself. You'll make it up next time the project goes out to bid.

That's the theory. Now, let us ask you a question. How many times have you ever successfully pulled off the we'll-make-it-up-next-time strategy? We didn't think so. Have you ever even met anyone who has pulled it off? It just doesn't work. Benjamin Franklin observed that the definition of insanity is doing the same thing over and over and expecting different results. We doubt Franklin ever got into price competition when he sold subscriptions to *Poor Richard's Almanac*.

Price competition is a fool's game because any fool can play it. In fact, weak competitors have an advantage in price competition because they've got little to lose and nothing else to leverage. New entrants to the market have to use low price, too, because they haven't yet proved their value to customers. Customers have discovered how to use price competition to their advantage. Customers qualify the low-priced vendors in order to get the high-value competitors to match the price. This book will show you how to avoid the trap of price competition.

Companies are not always aware that they have been trapped. We got an urgent telephone call from the VP of sales of a well-known electronics company. He wanted our advice on the best pricing strategy for a reverse auction in which the company was participating. A reverse or procurement auction is often used in industrial business-to-business procurements. It is a type of auction in which the role of the buyer and seller are reversed, with the primary objective to drive purchase prices downward. In a conventional auction, buyers compete to obtain a good or service. In a reverse auction, sellers compete to obtain business.

We had but one question for the VP of sales: Was his company the preferred buyer? The answer was no. Our advice was to get out of the auction. It was a waste of time for the company. There was no possibility of the company winning the order. In this scenario, the company was a rabbit. Its only role was to pressure the two preferred vendors to drop their prices.

What should the company have done instead? Our advice was to use the bid request as an opportunity to visit the company and talk to the engineering team or real decision maker about value. As for the two preferred vendors, they were trapped, too. Without knowing the identity of the third vendor, they would be operating at a significant disadvantage when the rabbit dropped its price.

Customers who switch to you for price will be the first to leave when another low-price competitor comes along. Price competition provides no sustainable competitive advantage unless it can lead a firm to take over an industry and only in the high-growth phase of a life cycle.

Do You Understand Your Value?

Value is the basis of business exchange. You provide products and services to customers so they can build their own value. In exchange, they take a part of that value you helped them build and return it to you in the form of price. That's the way business is supposed to work. Here's the million dollar question: Do you understand the value you provide for your customers? If you don't, how can you set prices rationally, much less have confidence in the prices you set?

If you don't understand the value you provide for your customers, the culprit is often a soft value proposition with no financial backup. The marketing department is fond of promoting soft value propositions ungrounded by real analysis. It is no wonder that salespeople disconnect from their marketing coworkers and customers want to commoditize what is offered. In too many cases, price is the only thing that customers can differentiate so price is the only thing salespeople sell.

Here's a statistic that may surprise you. Eighty-five percent of salespeople have never been exposed to the strategy or marketing plan of the firm. How can salespeople who do not understand the strategy of the firm hope to respond to customers and competitors? Some of this is because many firms often cannot define value or measure it. It's no wonder they focus on price. What other options are left?

An understanding and definition of value won't be enough. People in the organization need to believe in and be able to sell a uniform concept of value. We believe that the loss of pricing power stems from the combination of two factors. First is the inability of companies to understand the value of the products and services they deliver to customers. Second is the loss of confidence in their pricing strategy.

Price versus Value Focus

Companies that focus on providing tangible value to their customers are more profitable. That is not to say that other firms don't provide value to their customers. We see many firms in a wide range of industries provide high levels of value to their customers or their customers' customers. But often they don't recognize and focus on what this value delivers. Managers don't understand and focus on value so salespeople don't focus on value, either. If salespeople don't have value to focus on, they only have price to close a deal. The problem is that when a customer's purchasing agent asks for a lower price, salespeople often have little else to respond with than lower price.

One of our favorite clients is a national provider of products similar to electronic components. All of its competitors sell a commodity product. Almost everyone in this industry, including our client, focuses on price. Frankly, it's easier that way. It has a price—everyone has a price. Everyone tries to have the lowest price on a given day. Price negotiations are brutal. Margins are as thin as motel towels.

But our client decided to play by different rules. Two managers got tired of being victims of price. They decided to change how they thought about their business. They communicated differently. They innovated differently. And they partnered differently. First, the managers decided to shift their focus, which had been product-centric, to become customer-centric. This was a stark contrast to their competitors, who focused on producing products. In doing so, they realized they had to have a much better understanding of both how their customers used their products and how they could do a better job of meeting specific customer needs. They actively talked to their customers about their needs and made product and service improvements their customers valued. They elevated the conversation with customers from price to value, executed to the level of that value proposition, and made sure they charged for it. Rather than falling victim to the death spiral of price discounts, they were lifted by the rising cycle of value. And they helped their company become the fastest growing and most profitable in the industry.

Don't Bomb Your Competitors Back to the Stone Age

The two managers differentiated their business in another way. They put considerable energy into determining what their best customers were willing to pay for value. Their competitors traditionally focused their energies on providing immediate price quotes, monitoring industry prices, and matching the prices of competitors. This "bomb your competitors back to the stone age" approach dominated the industry. The result for the industry players was lower margins.

The two managers began setting prices based on the value they provided to their customers. If the value was higher, they charged for it. If the customer wanted a lower price, no problem. The managers just took away something of value from the offering, perhaps a delivery guarantee. This flexibility permitted the two managers to make money based on the way they provided their products and services—with varying levels of value. The net result was higher revenues and higher profits. We review the details of providing this flexibility in Rule Six, "Add New Products and Services that Give You Negotiating Pricing Flexibility and Growth."

When our client's competitors realized they were getting beaten despite occasionally offering lower prices, they began to give away some valued services to try to win back sales for their products. They knew the product was a commodity, but they hoped that by giving away services, they could close some business and differentiate themselves from our clients. The problem was that they were still focusing on price. Net result here was that their costs went up, eating further into profits, and they began to lose money. Eventually, the services themselves became commodities. By this time, the two managers were identifying new services to offer—and to charge for.

Any of our client's competitors could have done the same thing. The more competitors do this, the more likely that the industry as a whole can become more profitable. This is because sellers begin to train customers that if they want value, they have to pay for it. This was the case in the traditionally price-oriented automobile parts industry. When DaimlerChrysler started losing money, it began canceling contracts with its suppliers and asking for lower prices. The suppliers stopped shipping products, which shut the assembly lines down. Everybody was bruised. Many of the suppliers went out of business in the 1980s and 1990s. The surviving suppliers eventually learned that if they could regard themselves not just as a cost, but as a solution to help build value for the car companies, they could resist price erosion.

Tough Sales Negotiations

What happened to the tough sales negotiations we all get exposed to? The competitors continued to let those discussions focus on prices. The two managers set minimum prices and if the prices in the negotiations got below that level, they would walk away from the table. They also made sure that if they were competing against a competitor that didn't provide the service levels they did, they subtracted those services and adjusted prices to keep it apples-to-apples.

Perhaps the two managers were a little bit arrogant. But is that really a bad thing? It certainly is a heck of a lot better than the mindset of desperation that most managers have when it comes to thinking about their customers. When managers are desperate to close business, they lose the ability to pursue profitable business. This is because if managers are desperate to close an order and the customer asks for a lower price, they will give it to them each and every time. They have lost sight of their value and confidence in their price. As we explain in Rule One, we believe a little bit of arrogance is warranted.

The Customer Is Not *Always* Right

We all know the adage, "The customer is always right." The idea behind the saying was that the customer is always in the best position to define his or her requirements. Well, it wasn't true in the twentieth century, and it's certainly not true in the twenty-first. The greatest new products rarely flowed in response to articulated customer requirements. No customer told Xerox to build the copy machine. But Xerox took a risk and identified a market that few customers envisioned. More recently, no customer asked Sony to build a battery-operated product smaller than a wallet to play music. But Sony built the Walkman and only then did customers recognize its benefits. And even more recently, Apple repeated the same dynamic with the iPod. Customers were happy with Apple building computers. No one looked to it for managing and storing digital music. Today Apple derives more revenues from converged consumer devices than from computers. In January 2007 the company dropped the word *Computer* from its legal name.

Here's the lesson. Customers may not always be right, but they are always powerful. It's important to know the difference. It's especially important to know the difference when considering what customers expect from pricing. Over the years, customers have learned that if they ask for a lower price they will get it. In fact, customers have adopted a long list of tricks to get vendors to lower prices and then lower them again.

Salespeople are trained to be responsive to customers. This is a desirable attribute. But when a customer asks a salesperson to lower the price of a product, being responsive is not the same as automatically agreeing. When it comes to price, salespeople need to be responsive by asking questions and listening.

When customers ask for discounts, salespeople should turn the discussion to value. Customers expect this and typically attempt an end run on the salesperson. The customer telephones a senior manager at the salesperson's organization to rattle his or her cage in an attempt to get the manager to buy into the White Horse Syndrome. Sometimes the senior manager saves the customer the trouble by initiating the call. In either case, salespeople learn that when they try to hold the line on price, someone else in the organization will criticize them for messing up the sales opportunity. Salespeople quickly learn that they would be foolish to try to get additional profit for the company with higher prices. After all, aren't they paid to close deals, regardless of the costs for the company?

The real challenge is getting salespeople and managers to have more confidence in their pricing. This requires salespeople and managers alike to resist undermining prices with short-term, panic-oriented tactics. The bad news is that most companies do exactly that. The good news is that it takes just a few simple rules to reverse the process, build discipline into the pricing process, and stop leaving money on the table. In fact, the following 10 rules will lead to your pricing with confidence. Let's get started.

RULE ONE

REPLACE THE DISCOUNTING HABIT
WITH A LITTLE ARROGANCE

Discounting is a habit entrenched in most organizations. Simple analysis can point to where bad discounting leaves money on the table. Like any addiction, the discounting habit is tough to break cold turkey. The best way to dislodge any deep-rooted attitude is to replace it with another. Arrogance, just a little bit, signals the confidence needed to kick the discounting habit.

W e learned the danger of unthinking discounting when we started our first professional services business almost 15 years ago. There were only three of us then, and we did all the business development and proposal work ourselves. Then something happened, which led us to the rule: Replace the Discounting Habit with a Little Arrogance.

We got a call from a company that seemed to be interested in our services. So naturally we leapt at the opportunity and wrote a solid proposal with what we felt was fair pricing. The prospective customer responded by asking for a lower price. And when we lowered the price, he asked for a still lower price. After three cycles, we decided to change our approach. We then asked the prospect a question we should have asked in the beginning. "What do you know about us and how confident are you that we can solve your business problem?" His response was honest. "Nothing and not much."

That exchange led to a different conversation and a different proposal. The proposal focused on our understanding of the prospect's business pain, how our services would alleviate that pain, and how the prospect's business would directly benefit from the value our services added. A day later, with no more talk of discounts, the prospect gave us the engagement. From that exchange, we learned a critical lesson. If all you talk about with customers is price, there is no price that is going to be low enough. Price is important, but there are considerations that must come first. We learned to start the conversation with value.

When we started a new business four years ago, we received a call from a senior executive at a large electronics company. She wanted a quote to train and prepare a sales team for a negotiation with a tough price buyer that purchased over $1 billion of product from them. We asked what her budget was. When it was lower than our normal fee for such an activity, we did two things. First, we gave her the name of two consulting firms that could meet her budget, one in her immediate area. The second was to ask her a question. It was an important one: Was she thinking about this exercise as an expense or as an investment? She paused but answered honestly that she was thinking about it as an expense. That gave us a chance to talk about how it should be viewed as an investment and that there would be a probable payback on that investment. We booked the deal and went on to do a number of activities with that company.

Successful managers and salespeople know how they create value for customers and know how to change the discussion to value. The best companies know they have to display a little arrogance about the value they offer in order to send an important signal to potential buyers. That signal is: We are confident in the value we provide and, therefore, the prices we charge.

This attitude replaces the knee-jerk reaction of dropping price with the reaction of "Do you know what we offer?" Companies know that if they have one moment of weakness in the discussion with the customer, they will send the signal that there is a discount to be had. All the customer has to do is push for more. Instead, smart salespeople make trade-offs on the level of value a customer receives as part of the offering, to align with the customer's price. That little bit of arrogance is what gives companies the courage to demand a payback for the value they create for customers.

When your salespeople get asked for a lower price, what is their response? We suggest it *should* be some variation of "What do you know about us and how confident are you that we can solve your business problem?" Salespeople need to step back and ask a few questions about what business pain the customer is experiencing and what the customer is trying to accomplish. How does the business pain impact the customer's financial goals? How does it threaten relationships with their own customers? How does it limit the customer's opportunities? These questions should be asked at the beginning, with the implicit message that your company is in the best position among all other vendors to alleviate the customer's business pain. After that baseline is established, important conversations about pricing can take place. That's what we mean by replacing the discount habit with a little arrogance.

Arrogance, just a little, means that people, especially salespeople, feel confident about what their company offers and why it functions better on behalf of its customers. If they don't feel confident, how can you expect them to price with confidence? You're the victim we talked about in the introduction. If you don't have the arrogance, give up discounting for a while and go out and talk to customers. Talk to those who are using your products and services. Ask them a real simple question. Ask the question that you're afraid to ask because it may appear stupid: Why do you use our products? Listen real well to their answers. If these customers believe in your company, then maybe you had better believe in your company, too.

The starting point in being confident in your price is being confident in your value. That starting point begins at the top of the firm with the leadership and senior managers. If you want to stop any habit, you've got to replace it with something. If you want to replace the discounting habit, we recommend a couple of steps. First, recognize how bad it is. Once you realize how much money you're leaving on the table in your customer negotiations, develop some rules for when you will and won't discount. Start with your smallest, highest-value accounts and write those rules in stone. Notice the results. See, you didn't lose as many customers as you thought you would.

If You Don't Think You Can Control Price Discounting, You're Right

How many times have you felt the need to discount prices to meet your quarter or year-end sales objectives? Come on, be honest. We don't think that any of us can say "never" to the addiction of price discounting. When you have responsibilities to run a business, the pressure to keep the revenue flowing and people working is tremendous. That pressure is sometimes alleviated when markets are growing and customers are plentiful. But when industries slow down, as they inevitably do, the pressure to discount goes up exponentially.

There's nothing wrong with discounting. Sometimes it's the right response. It's the *habit* of discounting—the unthinking and throw-caution-to-the-wind desperation—that's so destructive. It's the addiction to discounting that we're against. The difficulty with discounting is, as with all addictions, that it is very difficult to stop. People get used to discounting. They defend it as "industry practice." Our clients tell us, "We have no choice but to discount because our competitors are nuts." In fact, the competitors just look like they are nuts because they have the same addiction. By the way, we always tell our clients, "Your competitors are saying the same thing about you, and for precisely the same reason."

Discounting never occurs in a vacuum. Companies and managers develop systems and processes that allow discounting to flourish. Discounting occurs despite vigorous attempts to control it.

Many companies have implemented systems that place barriers on salespeople who want to offer discounts. Managers do that because they think it limits the discounting. And it does, at first. Maybe the salesperson must first obtain the approval of a higher-level manager. In rare cases, the president of the company must sign off on discounting requests. But the systems usually fail and for the same reason: The systems are focused on approving and subsequently giving discounts. Everybody learns the game. Customers and salespeople alike play it well.

It's this discounting mindset that gives customers the entry point for obtaining discounts that are often not necessary to close the sale. We don't blame customers for negotiating for discounts. We blame the discounting habit. We've seen discounting justified in every possible way. Some companies justify it by customer. These companies start off by giving discounts to its largest customers "only." These are the big customers, perhaps the marquee opportunities in the industry, and they order lots of products and services. Perhaps the volume of business they transact legitimizes the discount, but perhaps not. But invariably the companies succumb to *discount creep*, the expansion of a project or mission beyond its original goals, often after initial successes. Then the midsized and smaller accounts start getting discounts, too.

Sometimes companies justify discounting by product. In these cases, discounts are offered only for commodity products with lots of competition. Again, discount creep kicks in. Pretty soon, the company's newer technology, innovative high-value offerings start getting discounted, too. Sure, there are some justifications, such as the ability to get the low-value commodity products put on the purchase order as well. But the results are the same. Companies end up leaving money on the table in the negotiating process.

The software industry is rife with examples of discounting run amok. Just before Oracle acquired PeopleSoft, both companies were offering discounts as high as 80 percent to close deals. The problem is that customers quickly figured out that it's in their interests to hold their orders to the very end of the quarter. Subsequently all of the business gets closed at a discount. To make matters worse, Oracle, the winner in the deal, blamed the problem on their customers: "... the tendency of some of our customers to wait until the end of the fiscal quarter or our fiscal year in hope of obtaining more favorable discounts."[1] Can a company's misfortunes in pricing ever be the customer's fault? We don't think so. Oracle simply trained its customers over time to expect large discounts.

Red Hat is a leading distributor of Linux-based software and services. The company recently reported 55 percent growth in revenue but missed the mark expected by analysts by 1.7 percent, causing a slight decline in the stock price. When questioned about this, Red Hat CEO Matt Szulik said, "Red Hat wasn't willing to yield on price just to close a deal at the end of the quarter. Why do something economically foolish to satisfy a near-term metric for Wall Street?"[2] Having set that expectation with customers, Red Hat's company performance continues to be solid. They have confidence in their pricing, and it shows in their growth, profits, and stock performance.

Who Gets and Gives Price Discounts?

Here is the first assignment in this book. Go ask for a plot of all of your customers' pricing. The plot can be for a high-value product or for a low-value one. It doesn't matter. If possible, have the summary reflect total discounts and total volume. For this first step, the goal is to show which customers are getting which discounts for which products. Ideally, the summary will also compare discounts for different sized customers.

Don't ask for data, ask for the plot. It's the graph that is worth a thousand words. Let's look at an example plot (Figure 1.1).

The plot represents the price charged per pound for a commodity product along with the total requirements for each customer. Notice several things about the plot. First, look at the number of customers who pay less than $0.30 per pound. That's 30 percent less than what the larger customers pay. Maybe the coding is wrong and the customer is actually buying a lot more than listed. Maybe it was a

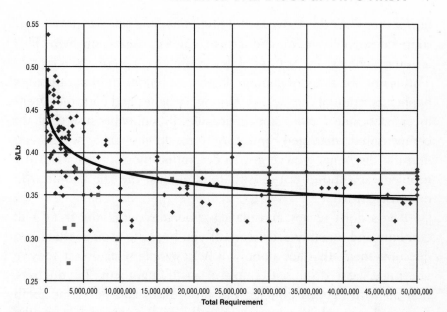

Figure 1.1   Prices Paid by Total Requirements.

sample order in the expectation that a customer was going to buy more in the future. Whatever the excuse, given that it is happening in so many accounts, this is a sure sign of uncontrolled discounting.

It also might be because a customer was given a quotation for a larger volume but is only purchasing a smaller volume at this time. This indicates poor control in executing quotations with customers. Whatever the reason, each of these dots has a story to tell and the story weaves a web of implications around the discounting for the firm. We continue to be amazed at the number of managers who fail to take advantage of the insights from this type of analysis. What gets measured gets done. If you review these plots and start to ask questions about who is getting discounts and why, you are going to find the problems that lead to excessive or just plain ad hoc discounting. Ask for the justifications for the discounts. Ask for the policies that control them. We predict you will not find such policies—that's the point of this exercise.

Take a look at who in the organization is giving the most discounts. Average the discounts for each of your salespeople. You will notice that some don't give lots of discounts. You will also notice that some salespeople and maybe sales managers give lots of them. This is going to be a scary process of discovery. Don't go on the warpath. This is not about apportioning blame. Just recognize that discounts happen because of the lack of training, systems, and controls. Well-meaning business professionals provide discounts because they are compensated, managed, and taught to do just that. When you find the discounts, you've got to determine the root causes of the problem, and those root causes are rarely just the salespeople who dispense them.

If you don't review and manage your discounts, the trend will continue and possibly accelerate. If you begin to look at them and question them, that act alone will help people realize that they've got to at least do a better job of justifying them. If you back that up with needed policies and procedures and put some teeth into implementing them, you are well on your way to kicking the discounting habit.

Be Willing to Fire Unprofitable Customers

Now that you know how bad your discounting is, you can begin to take proactive steps to repair the damage. One of the problems that leads to discounting is salespeople and managers who look for every opportunity to sell something. They don't stop and ask whether any particular customer or order is good or bad for the business. This is one of the root causes that leads to excessive discounting: selling to customers who don't and will never value the things you do as a firm. To make matters worse, these may be the customers who switch vendors, complain about everything, and extract all sorts of extra services that they don't pay for. Why do we continue to serve them? Because we are trained to satisfy the customers, whatever it takes. Whether it's smart—in other words, profitable—to continue to serve individual customers rarely enters the conversation.

We learned this lesson the hard way. Many years ago we started a project with a company that needed help with pricing a new product. Halfway through the project, we got a call from the purchasing agent at the client that he wanted to negotiate our fee down. We started to argue with him that reducing our fee would hurt the project, but he wasn't listening. All he cared about was his number. So we changed tactics. We agreed that we would be willing to renegotiate the scope and price of the project. In the meantime, we proposed that it would be best to shut the project down. The purchasing agent seemed okay with that.

Then we made a call to the senior vice president who had engaged us in the first place. Well, she was not so upbeat about shutting the project down. Within the hour, the purchasing agent was trying to reach us. We took an extra few hours to return his call, but within five minutes we had the project going again and at the price we wanted. The point is that you don't want to fire your customers; you want each one to be profitable. It's the willingness to fire them that makes the point and builds pricing power.

The correct response is to take a step back. Within the global view of possible markets, identify which customers and markets you cannot serve at a profit. If some customers are marginally profitable, but others are significantly more profitable, is your company better off serving the former, or are you better off focusing resources on the more profitable opportunities? It's a matter of defensive strategy. It's simply better for you that unprofitable customers are served by your competitors. It's one less burden for you and one more for them. It's important to determine which doors you do or don't want your salespeople knocking on. If you don't identify these doors, salespeople will waste their time and sell to customers that don't value your offerings. Unfortunately, the track record for business-to-business (BTB) companies in customer targeting and selection is not very good: 79 percent of BTB companies are undiscriminating, responding to all customers.[3] See Figure 1.2.

The 80/20 rule governs this discussion. Also known as the Pareto Curve, the 80/20 rule says that, on average, 80 percent of business

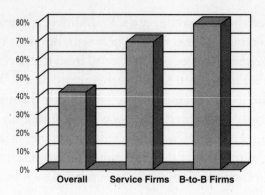

Figure 1.2 Percent of Companies that Respond to All Customers.

will come from 20 percent of customers. As a result, we tend to focus on the big customers who drive most of the business. We let distributors handle the 20 percent. Is this a good strategy? Not always. Research shows that big companies are more than twice as likely to be price buyers.[4] These customers are expert at draining every last drop of price discounts out of their suppliers.

To better highlight the problem, cost accountants have developed what they call the "20-225" rule.[5] Professors Cooper and Kaplan at the Harvard Business School have shown that once the cost of supporting customers is taken into account, only about 20 percent of customers are profitable. In fact, these 20 percent of customers account for 225 percent of the profits. Of course, this means that the other 80 percent of customers *lose* 125 percent of the profits. This principle applies equally to both private-sector and public-sector organizations.

The reality is that serving a large percentage of customers represents a loss for the business. The challenge, of course, is for a company to distinguish between the customers it can serve at a profit and those it cannot.

The first thing to do is select the low-hanging fruit. Make a list of all your customers, from the most profitable to the least. Focus on the 5 or 10 percent of your customers who are least profitable and fire them. These are the customers getting the big discounts but who fail to give you the big volume they invariably promised. These are the high-maintenance customers who the customer service department has on speed dial because they are so demanding. These are the customers who pay late. In other words, these are the customers who cost the company to service and keep on the books.

Firing them will do three things. First, it will increase your profits even though it may cost you some sales revenue at first. Second, it will send the signal to salespeople and customers alike that the company has pricing standards and is willing to stand by them. Your sales and customer service people will love you for it. Finally, it will free up your selling and service resources to pursue more profitable customers, who can add profits and revenue to the firm.

Because they are desperate for business, most managers don't want to fire customers. We don't like to do it either. The goal, of course, is to convert unprofitable customers into profitable ones. Before making a unilateral decision, we recommend that you have a candid conversation with the customers. Tell them why the relationship is not sustainable in its present form and let them know you are prepared to end the relationship. Some percentage of those bottom customers (larger than you may think) will understand and offer to keep doing business with you on some new terms. Only rarely is a customer's interests served by terminating relationships with trusted vendors. Sure, they will push you on price, and they will continue to push until you push back. Once they know they can't get any more concessions, most customers will work with you. And for the few customers willing to push you past the breaking point, let your competitors have the honor of serving them.

How Effective Are Your Price Discounts?

We had a business professor many years ago who said, "The essence of strategy is the efficient allocation of scarce resources so as to achieve maximum return." The point of that statement is that if you are going to do something as a manager, whether it is spending time, money, or both, for the sake of the company, you should have a basic understanding of what that expenditure is going to return in terms of added profits and added sales.

Of course, this is easier said than done. But look at the things you do. For example, you attend meetings to talk about new products or more efficient operations—two important activities designed to increase sales and profits. If you are going to give a price discount, don't you want to be sure that the discount drives added revenue and profits for the company? If you are with a large company, you know that research is conducted to determine market elasticity to changes in price. If markets are elastic, it means that sales are very responsive to changes in price. This can provide guidelines for determining how to get added revenue and profit. The problem is that those guidelines are often wrong.

We were recently contacted by a senior manager of a company to do consulting work. During one meeting, the client asked if we were qualified to do elasticity research. Our answer was "Yes, but elasticity research is not what you need." We could tell the manager wasn't used to being told that what he asked for wasn't really what he needed.

The reason for our position is that for business-to-business markets, elasticity research is rarely effective in driving pricing strategy. Price elasticity research tries to determine a market's responsiveness to changes in price. Elastic markets are quite responsive to changes in price. Inelastic markets are not. Elasticity research tells us when price decreases are going to bring us more revenue. This research also tells us when a price decrease means less revenue.

Now let's consider these layers of complexity when thinking about the use of elasticity research. There are three layers. The first layer is called *derived demand*. Derived demand says that demand for BTB products and services is derived from a downstream demand for your customer's products and services. That is true for original equipment manufactured (OEM) or maintenance, repair, or overhaul

(MRO) products, services, commodities, and high-value products as well. If demand is apportioned to something else, especially the activities in a different company's sales, it is not going to be responsive to changes in price. This makes it, by definition, inelastic. If you give a price discount, unit sales will be relatively fixed and revenue will go down. Profits? They eventually disappear. We talk more about this in Rule Three, "Apply One of Three Simple Pricing Strategies." The second layer is *customer behavior*. Some customers will change suppliers at the drop of a hat. They don't change their volumes—an attribute that elasticity research attempts to capture—but they switch back and forth between suppliers, usually driven by price. We call that *cross-elasticity of demand*. If we measure cross-elasticity of demand, we can determine a market's responsiveness to a company's changes in price, but it *is* unlikely that volume will change. That's because of the derived demand. This means that the elasticity we see isn't going to bring more volume into the market. We talk about this in Rule Four, "Play Better Poker with Customers."

Finally, you need to include *competitive behavior* into the mix. Unless you include competitors' willingness to respond and likelihood of responding, you are missing the most important element of the mix. Even if a market is elastic, when a competitor matches your price decrease, they negate any market effect. If your market is inelastic, as most markets are, you've just wasted a bunch of money on an elasticity study that misses most of the important elements of market dynamics. And you are led to believe that price discounts will work when they won't.

Dell profits are down because its price cuts have failed to spark sales of personal computers. Dell must be the only company in the U.S.–European PC business that thinks they can still do that. Understand that their fall from fame has been a slow affair, but the signal of it came in September 2006 when profits weren't what they expected.

Dell is learning what most other high-tech firms learned in the market downturn of 2000—that price cutting works if you have a cost leadership position in growth phases of market cycles. If you don't have the cost leadership position and/or the market slows down, you need to switch from a penetration prices strategy to a neutral one.

How can you tell? Look at the graph in Figure 1.3, which shows price discounting and gross sales growth. When one line starts heading up (discounting) and the other starts heading down (sales growth), it shouldn't take much more to signal that it's time to at least start thinking about changing your strategy. That's because you are trading profits for sales growth. Here, the leverage is lousy: For every dollar of revenue drop, you lose a dollar of profits. Profits disappear before revenue does. Long before. Dell's excuses are beginning to sound a little too familiar from quarter to quarter. As former Dell CEO, Kevin Rollins, said that Dell is "accelerating price adjustments." We don't know what that means. When companies move to neutral pricing strategy, it is a good idea to let other firms know. Confusing statements not only fail to do that but they actually will increase the price discounting by other companies.

If you don't have the resources of the big company, you still want to make sure it's worthwhile to investigate price effectiveness. Start with a simple plot of average discounts and sales growth on a year-to-year basis for at least four years like the one in Figure 1.3. The four years give you a trend line and the comparison of the two provides a good idea of the overall effectiveness of discounts

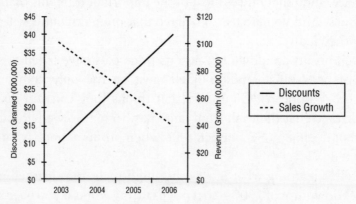

Figure 1.3   Discount Effectiveness, Four-Year Period.

and, perhaps more importantly, how that effectiveness is changing over time.

Notice in Figure 1.3 that discounts are increasing dramatically, yet sales growth is slowing just as dramatically. The price discounts are going up, but they are delivering fewer and fewer incremental sales for the same relative amount of discounts. This represents two things: increased competitiveness in the market and slowing growth of the primary market. It's a clear sign that the effectiveness of price discounting is declining. It's time to look for other ways to support the sale of the product. Promotion and improved sales skills are good areas to consider. There is one other thing clear in this plot. If the company isn't developing new products or technologies, they are going to see decreases in both sales volume *and* profits. More price discounts will not come close to solving that problem. In fact, it's only going to make things worse by sacrificing profits for sales that just aren't there.

Another thing to look at is a plot of revenue and unit sales growth for a product or service line. The graph in Figure 1.4 shows the effectiveness of price decreases to deliver more sales, but it does so by showing the end result of revenue. This equals price times units, that is, the sales volume.

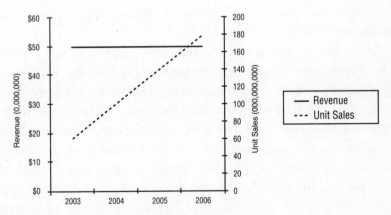

Figure 1.4   Unit Sales Impact on Revenue Growth.

Notice in Figure 1.4 that unit sales are increasing but the revenue is stable. This is indicative of a market that is just on the edge of maturity. Unit sales are still growing due, in part, to decreases in price. But the net effect is that revenue stays the same. Another way to say this is that despite decreases in price, unit volume is not coming up enough to make sales revenue grow. Normally, this would be a sign that it is time to stop giving discounts, but there is one interesting twist on this company's case: The technology was changing. This was actually a computer-based service. Due to increased sophistication in supporting technology to provide this service, costs were declining dramatically, too.

Managers took advantage of this insight by selectively offering price discounts to large customers in return for a long-term and higher share of their business. By doing this quietly, they were able to accomplish several things. First, they limited the likelihood that a competitor could react. Second, they were able to close out the competition with the long-term contracts. Finally, they were able to dramatically increase sales to the point that revenue was up roughly 15 percent and profits increased 35 percent, or roughly $35 million, from this simple insight. Not all discounts are bad—as long as you know where and how to give them. Even on the eve of a mature market, it's possible to use discounting effectively.

Let's look at one more plot (Figure 1.5) that points to the dramatic impact of "periods of desperation" that we talked about in the introduction.

What you see in Figure 1.5 is that every quarter, demand takes a spike. The reason is apparent in the quarterly drop in the average selling price for products. This is a sure sign of end of period desperation. Funny thing was that when we asked the senior executives if this was a problem, they said "No." The lower-level managers knew what was going on, but the senior managers didn't believe them. It was only when they saw this plot that they recognized they had a problem.

What was the fix? They adopted a system that simplified prices so everyone could see what was happening. They trained the

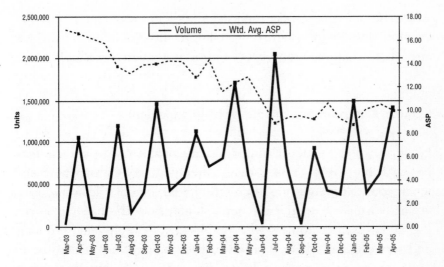

Figure 1.5 Monthly Discount Effectiveness.

salespeople about the value they had for their customers. They did have value—lots of it. They were the leading-edge technology supplier in this business. Sure, there were competitors. But the competitors' technology lagged by six to nine months, which was the window of time needed to have a higher price. The discounting was bad because it just pulled business up from the future month but at a lower price. No incremental business here. It was the graph of the bad behavior that showed the executive team they had an end of period discounting habit that had to be kicked. When they did kick it and were expecting a decline in sales, revenue actually increased 17 percent. Profits went up 37 percent, or roughly $300 million, money grabbed off the table by the right player.

Ask about your discounting practices. But, you've got to do more than just ask. You've got to dig into the responses and look at the graphs of the actual discounts to find out how bad it is. When you look at the graphs, make sure you understand them and begin to ask about the "outliers." This points to desperation pricers, so find out who they are and why they behave that way. There is one more way to see the face of a desperation pricer: Look in the mirror. Set a good example and begin to put some stakes in the ground around where and when to discount and, more importantly, when not to.

Control Discounting with Rules of Engagement

Now you know the depth of your pricing problem. The choices may be hard, but the process is easy. After your review of where and when your salespeople are discounting, you've got to decide when it is clearly a mistake to give discounts. It may be with small customers. It may be with customers who purchase your high-value products and services and where you have little competition. It may be in certain geographic markets. It may be with salespeople who haven't been through your value training program. You've got to identify where you are going to stop giving price discounts.

We call these *rules of engagement.* Simple rules of engagement are set to let salespeople and managers know that you are beginning to limit price discounts. And, you are willing to let some business go. If you have done a good job defining the rules of engagement, it shouldn't cost you much valuable business. By that, we mean you hopefully have identified the customers where it is wrong to be giving discounts. If they decide to leave, it is going to be good for your business. If a competitor takes them, it is great for you and the competitor suffers the deterioration of margins.

The trick to rules of engagement is to start with something easy. It's got to be something that everyone can understand and will agree that it's the next step. And, it's got to be something that you can put some teeth into. For example, consider organizing discounting dollars as a budgeted item. Each sales manager gets a bucket of discount dollars each quarter for his region. He must be careful to make them last for 90 days and that the right customers earn the right to the discounts allocated. Standards must be enforced. If you aren't willing to put teeth into the new rules of engagement, you're wasting your time. Sales managers will just keep asking to get their buckets refilled. Sure, if you feel like blustering about discounts go ahead, but unless you are willing to enforce your new policy, you are better off doing what you were doing before. We know of one company that on a yearly basis fires their most extreme discounters. This kind of "rank-and-yank" strategy has other costs, but it definitely sends a message about what the organization values.

Notes

1. Oracle 10-K, June 25, 2004.
2. Stephen Shankland, "Red Hat Pulls Out a Profit," c/net news.com, December 22, 2004.
3. Lion Arussy (2005). *Passionate and Profitable: Why Customer Strategies Fail and Ten Steps to Do Them Right*, Hoboken, NJ: John Wiley & Sons.
4. Reed K. Holden (1990). *An Exploratory Study of Trust in Buyer-Seller Relationship*, Boston: Boston University.
5. Robin Cooper and Robert S. Kaplan, "Profit Priorities from Activity Based Costing," *Harvard Business Review* Onpoint, April 15, 2000, Cambridge, MA.

Understand the Value You Offer to Your Customer

You can't have confidence in your pricing until you have confidence in the financial value that your offerings create for customers. Even though many managers are convinced they can't get this information, the reality is that most of your customers are eager to tell you. All it takes is asking the right questions and being willing to listen.

I n the pricing seminars we lead, we often start with this question: "How do you win at poker?"

The best poker players win by being good at bluffing. Every price negotiation game has an element of bluffing. Both customers and suppliers do it, but the customer usually has an advantage because his bluff—walking away—is more credible. It's a bluff that few sales professionals want to risk. Customers know this and use it to their advantage. Salespeople respond with lower prices because they are afraid of the consequences—a lost customer—if they don't. In short, they lack the confidence that their pricing strategy is sound. They lose sight of the important value they offer to the customer. Salespeople forget that this is all just a poker game. They take the safe route and offer a discount. The customers gleefully sweep the money off the table. They do it because they know how to bluff.

There are two elements of a bluff. First is when you don't have a good hand. In this case, bluffing is all you can do to win. It's gutsy poker and based on a wing and a prayer. And, if you're up against a customer who has a better hand, you'll lose every time. You shouldn't run a business or play poker this way. Fortunately, the best bluff is when you've got a good hand. Here, your challenge is not to get bluffed off the table by someone who has a worse hand. This is a much better way to play poker. But, you've got to be confident in that hand just like you've got to be confident in your price. The goal of Rule Two is to find out if you've got a good hand and if that hand is good enough to win against a bluff. It's here that you must have confidence in your prices so you don't fold your hand and discount when a buyer bluffs you.

The goal of this rule is to get you to understand your value to your customer. If you can do that, it's almost like you are able to see the customer's hand. The customer's capacity to bluff is eliminated. We believe that pricing with confidence allows you to play a pricing hand as if you could see your opponent's cards. When you play a hand differently from the way you would have played it if you could see the others' cards, you leave money on the table. When you play a hand the same way you would have played it if you could see all their cards, the money on the table is yours.

The goal of Rule Two is to help you win every pricing hand and stop leaving money on the table.

Winning the Pricing Game

The key to winning the pricing game is to (1) create a range of low- to high-value offerings, (2) provide quantifiable value propositions and sales tools that define value at the level of the individual account, and (3) create pricing strategies and price levels that capture a fair share of the value that you create. Do these things well and pricing confidence soars. When everyone in the organization knows that you have the right offerings and that your prices are right, the sales team regains control of the negotiations. This all rests on a solid understanding of the value that your products and services already do or could create for your customer.

There is one major challenge in achieving this vision. How many times have you heard an executive say, "We want to provide the best value for our customers"? It's a common statement. But what exactly does it mean? Does the company intend to deliver a lot of customer benefits but at prices that are similar to the competition? Or does it mean that the company is going to offer what everyone else in the industry offers but at the lowest prices? Or that it is going to meet customer needs and hope that it will get some payment for it? The problem is that the word *value* in this context is so general that it has no meaning. Companies that lack a clear definition of value to the customer cannot negotiate effectively. After all, how can you build your pricing confidence around a concept that you yourself cannot define?

Sometimes our clients object that it is not for the company to determine value. Value, this objection continues, must be defined by each customer, and it stands to reason that each customer defines value uniquely. In other words, the customer is always right. By this formulation, the company must react to the definition of value imposed by each customer. In the poker game of buying, that value is often a bluff.

We reject this formulation. We think it's a cop-out. It's not a question of right and wrong. Our experience is that firms that pursue this strategy lose focus and see margins decline. Moreover, they incur unnecessary selling costs as they attempt to figure out what each customer's approximation of value is. One word describes the result of this approach. That word is *confusion*, because every customer's need becomes an undifferentiated priority.

With Rule Two we'll help you avoid this confusion by focusing on the most important definition of value in business-to-business markets. The result is clarity in the financial benefits that your offerings create for your customers. We'll also show you some deceptively simple techniques for uncovering this goldmine of information—information that the most sophisticated market research approaches often fail to uncover. Finally, we'll show you how to put these insights to practical use in developing strong value propositions and effective tools for your sales teams—tools that are essential for positioning and defending your prices.

The One Definition of Value that Matters Most

There are all kinds of value. We are referring exclusively to *financial* value. More specifically, financial value refers to profits that result when costs are subtracted from revenues. Regardless of how customers talk about the subject, in a business-to-business context, dollars that fall to the customer's bottom line when it uses your offering is the true measure of financial value. Businesses are profit-making entities. Their actions and who they purchase goods and services from are driven by a desire to improve profits. They accomplish this by purchasing from suppliers that excel at helping them meet their profit goals. The equation is simple: Decrease your customers' total costs and/or increase their revenues and you increase their profits. Now we're talking about a definition of value that everyone understands.

If you lack the ability to connect what benefits your offering delivers to how it will improve profits for your customers, you are operating at a huge disadvantage. If you can't articulate your value in dollars and cents, you won't get paid for it. Let us tell you about one of our clients that benefited from analyzing financial value to its customers. This company analyzes its offerings to understand its value positioning with customers. It sets prices and negotiates based on this understanding. After rolling out this value-based approach, it has seen its market share *and* its margins increase. This company, as you might expect, is not a niche player or a provider of a highly differentiated offering. Both of these situations facilitate value positioning. No, actually the company that we are talking about sells dirt.

Dirt! How could the company possibly differentiate itself or position its product? The company invested in *services* that enable its customers to reduce delays at the job site. The company understood that its customers determined the value provided by its dirt vendor not so much by the quality of dirt provided but *how* the product was provided. The company saw that if it could help its customers eliminate delays caused by the delivery of dirt, the customer would reduce costs and get paid faster. The company created scenarios that demonstrated precisely how much customers' operating costs would decrease using its service. Customers responded by selecting the company because it made the connection to increased profits unmistakable. The company now commands a slight premium in the ultimate commodity business.

Adopting a Value Mindset

The key to unlocking all of these benefits lies with your organization's ability to understand how your offerings create financial value for your customers. Understanding value comes from a process that should be familiar to just about everyone in your organization: asking customers questions about their business. We're not necessarily talking about big, complex research projects here. The best insights often come from your feet in the street. That can mean salespeople, but it can also mean service people and senior executives. Anyone who has contact with a customer, if properly trained, can have a research mindset. They can learn from that customer. These opportunities for education can have a highly beneficial impact for your own firm.

There is one question that we do not recommend you ask your customers. And that is, "What do you think of our prices?" Asking customers directly about your prices is an invitation for them to posture. Everyone will agree that your prices are too high. Is that surprising? Your customers have every incentive to try to get you to believe this. The better questions center on their requirements, the benefits provided by your offerings, and how the two interrelate. The key is to understand your value to your customers and then use this to manage their willingness to pay. By showing that you understand your value and demonstrating that your prices are reasonable given that value, you change the discussion. It is no longer just about price but about value and price.

Some of our clients are tempted to ask their customers if they are satisfied with your prices. This question also is a mistake. The truth is you don't want customers to be totally satisfied with your prices. If a customer is satisfied, your prices are likely too low. A better scenario is when customers acknowledge that your prices are fair or reasonable. If you sell high-value products with lots of service and support, you might want customers to acknowledge that, yes, your prices are high, but on the whole you are worth it.

Why Talk to Customers about Value?

Judging by the way many companies research their customers, the question "Why talk to customers about value?" is not merely rhetorical. Managers spend a lot of time and money researching customer attitudes and needs. Unfortunately, most of this research fails to answer two fundamental questions. The first is "What is driving these attitudes and needs?" The second is "What are the implications (for both us and the customer) of addressing them?" By answering these two questions, we can answer an even more fundamental one: "Where do we provide value to our customers?"

Without answers to these questions, companies are adrift. Businesses want to focus their resources on the best opportunities to provide financial value to their customers. And they especially want to concentrate on cultivating those areas where the business value proposition can be differentiated. Gaining insight in these areas can have a profound impact on any business. It positions businesses to create more valuable offerings, to target the best customers for those offerings, and to empower their sales organization to sell value and defend prices.

To have confidence in pricing, it is critical to understand some fundamental aspects about customers, their businesses, and what it is they value. You can use these insights to achieve a number of agreeable outcomes. The insights pave the way for better segmentation and targeting and the creation of offerings that are deemed by the customers to have value. The insights also serve as the foundation for well-defined price-value trade-offs, better value positioning, and better pricing. Figure 2.1 summarizes the power of understanding your value to your customer.

The progression of questions and objectives in Figure 2.1 underscores an unexpected point: Any knowledge of the value you deliver to your customers gives you greater control over, and confidence in, your pricing. What's unexpected is that it addresses pricing as part of a progression that includes marketing strategy, product management, and sales strategies and techniques. It is with these activities that we create and frame our value to our customers. When firms apply their understanding of customer value in this way, positioning prices as fair relative to the value provided is quite simple.

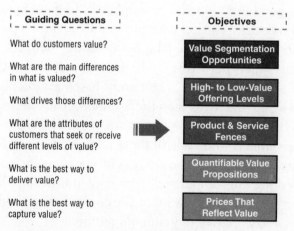

Figure 2.1   The Power of Understanding Customer Value.

Customers Want to Talk about Value

One of the objections most frequently raised when we recommend asking customers about how they define value and how a supplier contributes to it goes something like this.

> Why would our customers share this kind of information with us? They'd be crazy to talk to us about how they make money and how our offerings help them make more of it. Won't they be afraid we would use that information against them? Won't they see this as a ruse to get them to give us the justification to raise our prices?

Our experience is that these objections are not the norm. The customers, of course, have to have some basis for trust. And you must demonstrate that you are sincere in collecting the information for their ultimate benefit. In other words, if your attitude is that this information will help you help them run their own businesses more efficiently, then your customers may welcome the conversation. It turns out that most customers are eager to talk about their businesses, their goals, and their efforts to be successful. Their motivation for doing so is simple and clear. The more their suppliers understand their business issues, the better able those suppliers will be to craft solutions that are relevant and valuable.

It takes good listening and probing skills to gather this information. It also requires shifting your internal view (how you think you perform) to an external view (the performance, benefits, and value that your customers perceive). Only the latter view counts. This is a significant problem in many technology-based product and service companies where the focus is on the features of the offering. This is a process to convert the internal view into one that is more important to customers, that is, the value of those features to them. Finally, the analysis has to be done in the context of your specific competitors. Customers don't think about your company in a vacuum. When they think about you at all, it's always in the context of how you perform on any given day relative to your competitors.

One of our clients produces heavy equipment. Its value challenge was that there was little differentiation between its products and that of the competition. As much as 80 percent of the components in their major products were common to the products of the competition. Given this commonality, the industry was racked by intense price negotiating. Our job was to interview the client's customers to determine if there were points of differentiation we could leverage.

Over the course of the first six interviews, we gained enough information to show our client that on a number of dimensions, it provided demonstrably more value than the competition. When our client's most important customers talked about what they appreciated about our client's business model, they had a common response: They benefited from the value of our client's dealer network. This dealer network was almost twice as large as the next largest supplier. The customers saw over and over again how the scale of the dealer network reduced downtime, decreased operating costs, and kept revenue-producing assets in the field. For example, if a customer needed a critical part and its local dealer didn't have any in inventory, the part could be obtained very quickly from another dealer in the network. With just a handful of interviews, we learned that our client's customers perceived an incremental value of 15 to 20 percent buying from our client compared with buying a similar product from the competition. Our client used that information to focus its marketing efforts and defend its prices.

How Does the Customer Get Financial Value from the Use of the Offering?

The trick is to drive the discussion to a dollar sign. If you can't focus on the financial value, any talk about value to the customer is just noise. You've got nothing to back up the talk (Figure 2.2).

We were working with a company that offered a wireless infrastructure solution. During their initial internal discussions, the

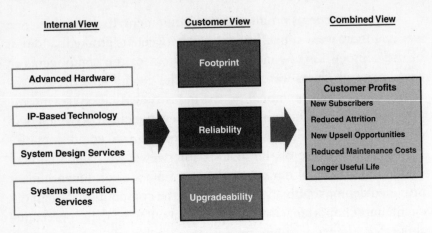

Figure 2.2   Connecting Features to Benefits to Value.

information technology (IT) and services people focused exclusively on the technology of the product. Now, these are fine people who make an important contribution to the solution, but their comments focused on the technology, process, design, and integration services that they delivered to their customers. These things *are* important, but they are not the first things the customer wants to talk about. Customers are more concerned about geographical coverage of services, uptime, and reliability of the platform. We were engaged to coach the supplier team. It took only a three-hour meeting to show the team how each of the features that the technical staff focused on aligned with the benefits that the customers wanted and what the subsequent financial results were to the customer. Once they identified a combined view, they all understood each other.

The financial connection comes from a process we call *drilling down* during the internal and external interview process. Drilling down is the tactic of probing to uncover the details underneath the customer's first answer, which is often superficial. The drill down generates critical value insights because it moves well beyond the cursory answers that most customer research provides.

This approach provides more precise measures of financial value by measuring your offering's direct impacts of reducing costs, improving efficiencies, and increasing revenue opportunity. For example, you may be selling a $10 device that is critical to the performance of a $1,000 product. In attitudinal research, value is determined by comparing perceived attributes of the $10 device. Attitude research would show a value improvement of only $1, resulting in lots of money being left on the table. A 10 percent improvement in the performance of that device *can* create hundreds of dollars of value of performance for the products in which it is installed. The goal is to determine the impact of the performance of the entire product—thus revealing much more value than you would expect.

Figure 2.3 is an actual transcript of a series of questions we asked a client's customer when we were training a client team on how to conduct this type of research. The respondent was the executive vice president of a $1 billion systems integration company.

The initial question was "What do you really need from us?" The response: reliable messaging. When we asked the executive why reliable messaging was so important, he answered that 50 percent of the company's technical support budget would be saved if the company had reliable messaging. The bottom line is that we were

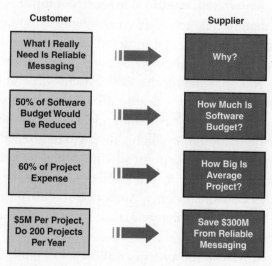

Figure 2.3   Drilling Down on Customer Value.

able to determine that if they had reliable messaging in their software tools, the firm would save $300 million in technical support and software development expenses. That is quite an opportunity to provide a quantifiable return on investment (ROI) for selling the right offering.

Was it hard to do that? Not really. It took curiosity and a willingness to ask simple questions and then listen. One of Stephen Covey's seven habits of leadership is to seek to understand before seeking to be understood. This process is not difficult for those firms that want to do a better job of understanding their customers. However, many managers find themselves too bogged down in day-to-day activities to accomplish these tasks with customers in mind. We often find that the reason for this is because it's easier for managers to use anecdotal stories from customers rather than digging into customer value research.

Overview of the Process

An effective conversation with a customer requires preparation; the goal is to ask penetrating questions in search of insights that are not always immediately clear to either you or your customer. Customers don't always think about value in detail. You need to be prepared to pose specific questions about value and let the customer respond. In doing so, you are framing the value discussion and challenging the customer to think more deeply about their true value needs. To do this, you need to have some clear ideas about how your offerings create value *before* talking to customers. Otherwise, you won't recognize a promising point when it comes up and you'll miss the chance to drill down on it. The good news is that the preparation itself generates valuable insights. And once you learn the process, it is very easy to repeat (see Figure 2.4). It's a good skill for managers to learn.

When you follow the process outlined in Figure 2.4, you are creating the foundation for confidence in pricing. You can use your

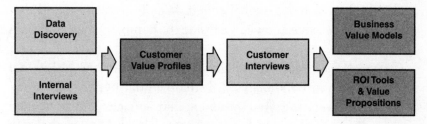

Figure 2.4 The Customer Value Research Process.

customers' own words and data to prove your value. And when you prove your value, you can show that your pricing is thoughtful and stands up to the scrutiny of hard-driving customers. First, let's look at the process; then we'll look at the actual interview preparation in more detail.

1. *Data Discovery:* Sales and marketing departments are drowning in reports and data. The problem is that they don't know what to do with them. The first step of profiling customers is to put all of that data into a big pile or data file. If necessary, plot the data to get those insights. Look at each file and understand, at a high level, what it is telling you about your customers. Summarize each file and the key insights. In particular, you are looking for:
   - Specific examples that connect your offerings to financial benefits for customers
   - Insights into your customers' profit models and their positioning with their customers
   - Direct comparisons with your competition
2. *Internal Interviews:* Talk with sales, marketing, and services executives in your company. They know how customers use your products and services. Ask them to detail how and why customers use your current offering and how that offering creates value for them. Also, push for meaningful comparisons to competitors and what the ultimate financial benefit of the difference is to customers. An important element of this process is to ask for proof whenever anyone makes an assertion about how customers view you and your competitors. Never let blanket statements or

accepted wisdom go unchallenged. We almost always find that there is more value knowledge inside the company than managers realize.

3. *Customer Value Profiles:* Given what you've learned from the internal interviews and data analysis, develop initial hypotheses about how customers use your products and services and how they get value from that use. In this process, you'll discover that you understand far less than you think. Remind yourself that the whole point of the process is discovery. Note critical gaps in your information and identify which customers can help you fill those gaps. Develop a list of questions to ask customers about how you perform relative to competitors.

4. *Customer Interviews:* Customer interviews are used to validate and/or discredit the value profiles identified with the internal analysis. Use customer interviews to develop new value profiles. The method used to determine customer value profiles is *depth research,* which we discuss in the next section. This method accomplishes two primary tasks. First, it provides a much richer understanding of how customers use your products or services and how to improve them. Second, it is a bit like therapy for customers. They finally have someone from the company to talk to in depth who makes them feel they are important customers. The very process of the interview improves the relationship. If you use the insights to improve products and services, it's a win-win for everyone.

5. *Business Value Models:* After the customer interviews are documented and read, you begin to develop an understanding of a common thread between different customers within a segment. That common thread can be in their business models, how they run their business, or how they can achieve value from using your firm. At this point you should be able to map out how your customers make a profit, how your offerings help in that process, and have a number of specific examples to back up your ideas. The goal at this stage is not perfection. The point is to draw connections between pieces of data gathered from different customer conversations.

6. *ROI Tool and Value Propositions:* The final result of all this work is two things. First is a series of strong value propositions that salespeople will be able to use to sell your products and defend your price. Second is an ROI tool salespeople can use to ask a number of qualifying questions to determine if there is a need for your offering and how that offering will subsequently provide financial value for customers.

Preparing for and Conducting the Interview

It's worth spending a few moments to talk about conducting the actual interview.. The better prepared you are for the process, the more likely you will be to glean the right pieces of information and follow the right threads to financial value. There are three distinct steps to think about: preparation, execution, and integration. The technical term for the actual interview is *exploratory depth research.* It is exploratory in that it uses your insights to develop hypotheses about how your customers value your products and services. Through multiple interviews, you can either confirm or revise the hypotheses. It is a depth approach in that probing techniques go beyond superficial answers. It gets to what real points of pain your customers have and what they value when looking for a solution. This approach drills down with a series of simple questions to find out how product or service features reduce costs or increase prices and sales. It identifies the real *value drivers* of a business.

When doing depth research with a client's customers, we find:

1. The real drivers of customer value are somewhat different than the selling firm expected.
2. The current solutions are more valuable than estimated by the supplier.
3. Customers are pleased that someone is finally asking them about their business in a meaningful way.
4. There are opportunities to provide much more value than suppliers currently offer.

In preparing for the interview, your job will be to link together three specific areas: the customer's profit model, their key revenue and cost drivers, and critical performance measures (often called *customer value drivers*). The big question is, how do they grow their business and make money? In other words, how can *you* help them grow faster and make more money? The second is to connect your offering and those of your competitors to these measures. The third step is to define specific financial results that your offerings have delivered for your customers. That's what we did with the systems integrator in Figure 2.5. To do that, we had to connect these three areas by asking simple questions.

The interview process takes three distinct steps: preparation, execution, and integration. It is a straightforward process and can be easily adopted by marketing managers.

The preparation step uses the internal information from the data review and stakeholder interviews to develop ideas about the customer's value drivers. It comes to initial conclusions about your own performance as well as the performance of your competition against those value drivers. Customer interview selection criteria are developed as well, for example, What industry segment do you want to

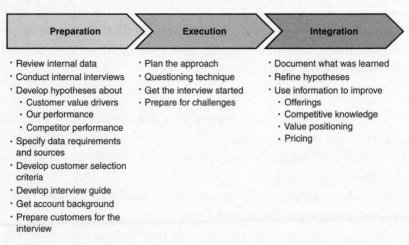

Figure 2.5   The Customer Interviewing Process.

review? What size customers do you want to serve? What customers already think like this?

When you call customers to set up the interview, it's a good idea to tell them that the purpose of the interview is to develop a better understanding of their business and what their real needs are. Be clear that you are there to listen and not to sell anything. Repeat that last promise. This is not a sales call. And, having made that promise, take care to honor it. Nothing will undermine the interview more than the slightest hint that it's a sales call in disguise. Also, try not to ask for such interviews when the customer is in the middle of a request for proposal (RFP) or a sales negotiation. They'll be too focused on posturing for a discount.

Once the hypothesis is developed, the next step is to develop an interview guide. This is a template for a series of questions designed to either support or invalidate the hypotheses. Keep the guide simple. Direct, open-ended questions and short words are good guidelines to develop the guide. Keep it to one page. That's a hard-and-fast rule. If you need more than one page to test the hypothesis, the hypothesis is too complicated. It's probably two or more hypotheses combined into one. Break it up into its constituent pieces and, if necessary, test each one.

Figure 2.6 lists fundamental questions that will help you get started.

At the start of the interview, tell the respondent why you are there and ask easier questions up front. Questions should be short and to the point. Just as you aren't there to sell anything, let the customer know that you aren't there to answer or respond to any questions or problems with products or services. Take notes on any issues the customer brings up and say that you or someone else will follow up at a later time.

During the interview, follow the leads that the customer provides. As we've already discussed, this process is called the *drill down*. We use this term because of the increasingly specific nature of your questions as you move from broad business issues to the real point: dollars and cents data on value. You will want to start with some higher-level

---

Strategy
- What is the customer's profit model? How do they make money?
- What are the critical success factors for the customer?
- What are the critical processes for their business?
- What keeps them awake at night?

Revenues
- Where is the customer's value add for *their customers*?
- How are they positioned in the market?
- Which markets/applications drive the most revenue?
- Which markets/customers are seen as the future?

Costs
- What are the major line items in their P&L?
- What drives costs into or out of their operations?
- Are there critical areas for improvement?

Our Offering
- How are our offerings used in their business?
- What offerings are most valuable to the customer? Why?
- What specific results do our offerings help the customer achieve?

Competition
- Who is the next best competitive alternative? Why?
- What is it that they bring to the table that we cannot and vice versa?
- What sacrifices are associated with using the various alternatives?

Figure 2.6 Customer Interviews—Guiding Questions.

questions and then use increasing focus to unearth specific data on how you and your competitors create financial value for the customer. An overview of the drill down is shown in Figure 2.7.

Once the interview is over, two things need to happen. First, document what you learned from the interview. Ideally, you have notes or even a transcript from the interview. Take 30 minutes and turn those notes into a document that can be used to make compelling points to other managers. Second, send a thank-you note to the customer. We think a real letter signed by the chief executive of your company, with a copy to the CEO of the customer, is a classy way to go. An e-mail may work as well.

The next step is to transform the information from the interview into knowledge that your company can act on. Knowledge is actionable information. Summarize the key points and insights of each interview. If you have some specific customer quotes, use them

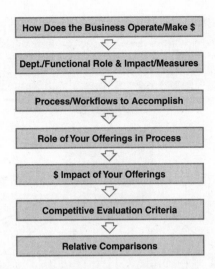

Figure 2.7   Drilling Down during Customer Interviews.

to make your point to internal executives during the readout of the results. The important thing is to keep track of your insights on customer value drivers, possible value positioning, competitive value positioning, pricing, and possible product or service enhancements. This library is powerful reading and should be kept up to date to help create case studies to support your value over time.

We helped a supplier of business forms conduct this process in the banking industry. At the time, this supplier offered 150 individual services on an ad hoc basis to its customers. Many of these services were provided on request without charge. Based on the customer interviews, our client discovered that a majority of the banks identified a specific bundle of these services as especially valuable. The client was further amazed that the bundle of services cut across a number of banking segments that were otherwise very different in their business models. In fact, they found that they could dramatically simplify their service offering and start charging for those bundled services. Clearly, the client was leaving money on the table by not recognizing the value of these services.

As a result of these insights, the client rationalized the bundle into 10 segmented service packages, each priced accordingly. The

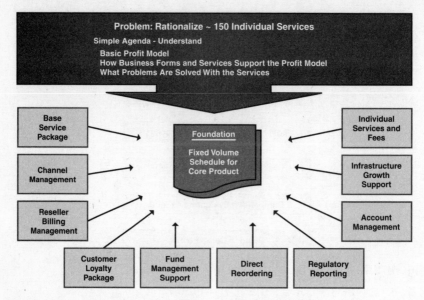

Figure 2.8   Using Customer Value to Simplify Offerings.

offerings also included a bare-bones basic service package (see Figure 2.8). When the services were rolled out, the supplier reversed a 5 percent per year decline in profitability and began growing at 5 percent per year in a declining business. Much of this success can be attributed to the fact that the connection between the customer's business model and their high-value needs was easy for the sales force to implement. All sales had to do was ask each prospect a couple of questions about their business and how they planned to grow it. With the answers to these questions, the account representative was able to quickly move to selecting the best offering for the customer and position it with concrete statements about its value.

What to Do with the Results of Your Conversations

It's exciting to talk to your customers about how your offerings provide value. At the start, it can also be a bit overwhelming. You are learning so many new things and are so involved looking for patterns in what you discover that it can be easy to lose sight of what you are trying to accomplish. Just remember, your goal is to develop simple models that enable you to quantify the value that you deliver to your customers. With this information, you can then:

1. Define offerings that clearly connect to customer value needs.
2. Define high-to-low value offerings to meet different price points.
3. Create high-impact value propositions and tools that enable your sales teams to win more deals and defend prices.
4. Set price levels that correlate with value delivered to the customer (see Figure 2.9).

Let's look at how this can play out. We were approached by a leading manufacturer of dental equipment. The company had an innovative breakthrough that promised dentists a cost-effective set of disposable dental products to replace products that dentists had to sterilize. Interviews with dentists revealed the considerable value many practitioners associated with eliminating the labor-intensive and risky sterilization process. Working with dentists, the interviewers determined that disposable products improved procedure room utilization by reducing clean-up time. Dentists were able to handle more patients, thus increasing their income. It also provided a market opportunity for oral surgeons seeking to differentiate themselves by

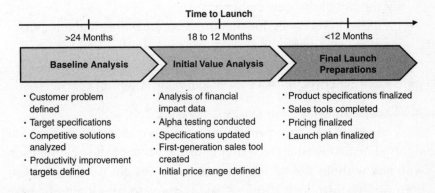

Figure 2.9 Customer Value Drives Product Positioning and Pricing.

advertising that they use the safest and most advanced equipment. Thus they could attract even more patients. Finally, the company was able to provide a simple billing software solution to connect the use of the equipment to specific patients and procedures. The software improved billing accuracy and reimbursement realization for those patients using dental insurance. This helped the dentists leave less money on the table.

Using this information, the dental products company established pricing by following a three-step process.

1. Determine the total costs to the customer of their current solution options.
2. Define the financial benefits that your innovation delivers *over and above current alternatives*.
3. Define the switching costs for customers that want to move to your solution.

In the case of our dental equipment manufacturer, that meant determining the following:

- The cost per procedure of current solutions by amortizing the total lifetime costs of current, reusable equipment over the number of procedures performed.
- The cost savings due to greater procedure room utilization.
- The incremental revenue from patients attracted to the practice by the use of the new equipment.
- Increases in revenues due to more accurate billing and reimbursement management.
- The cost savings due to reductions in procedure data entry.
- Switching costs, in this case disposal and training costs.

Their findings are summarized in Figure 2.10.

The results of customer value research yield two important insights. The first is an understanding of the value of the new solution with and without the billing software. This insight points to an opportunity to introduce a higher-value complete solution and a base solution that does not include the software.

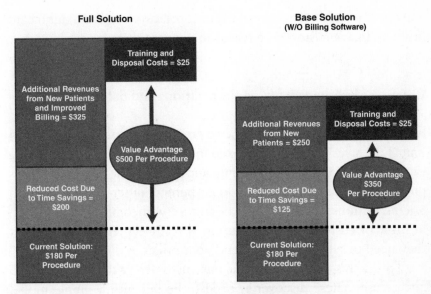

Figure 2.10   Business Value Models for a New Dental Instrument.

It also defines the basis for pricing by defining customer value. Knowing this value helped the firm establish a price range that captured a fair share of the value created for customers. To do this, it first defined its value advantage over existing solutions (in this case, $500 per procedure for the full solution and $350 for the base solution). Next it added the cost of the current solution to define the maximum range of price options available: $180 to $680 (the $180 cost of the current solution plus the $500 value advantage) for the full solution and $180 to $530 for the base solution.

To narrow down this range, the company analyzed the psychological elements of value from the customer's perspective. This included negative perceptions such as risk by adopting the new technology and concerns about moving from the demonstrated solution to something untried. It also included positive psychological benefits such as pride in operating on the cutting edge. Finally, they needed to set a price that offered *some* incentive to purchase. At the end of the process, the company decided on a price of $400 per instrument for the full solution and $250 for the base solution. While at the lower end of the possible range, even the base solution ensured a significant profit and gave customers a reasonable incentive to switch.

Creating High-Impact Value Propositions and Sales Tools

Even though what we have done so far is interesting, it is a waste of time if the sales force is overlooked in the process. Just documenting value and using it to define offerings and prices are not enough. If sales professionals can't defend the logic behind different offering and pricing options, then they will be in a very uncomfortable position in front of customers. The solution is to give them the tools that they need to sell value and defend your prices.

To do this, we need to put our customer value discoveries to further use. These discoveries need to be put into a simple model to show how customers get value from your offerings. This provides a structure of questions for your salespeople to ask your customers in order to determine how your products and services financially impact the customer's business on a case-by-case basis. Figure 2.11 shows what the structure of such a tool looks like.

Unfortunately, most ROI tools that marketers provide to salespeople don't work. The major reason they fail is that salespeople find

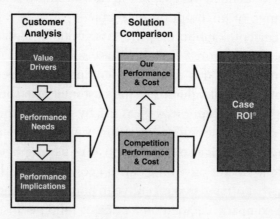

Figure 2.11   Structure for Credible ROI Tools.

them too complicated and therefore don't use them. Another reason is that a significant number of customers who go to the trouble of doing the analysis don't trust the results.

The solution is to develop sales tools that use the customer's own data. The analysis should provide explicit consideration of competitive alternatives. The objective is to make the customer's purchasing decision easier, not harder by hiding information from them. Presenting data that gives direct visibility to your competition can seem counterintuitive to many sales professionals. After all, why invite comparison and strengthen the customer's negotiating position? The fact is that comparing your products with those of competitors highlights both strengths and weaknesses. Balanced selling actually improves the credibility of salespeople.

In addition to issues of credibility, there is another important difference. Traditional ROI modeling often provides data on the average customer, aggregated at some level for a group of customers. Detailed comparison is left in the hands of the customer who may not judge accurately or fairly. Providing a case-by-case comparison ensures that sellers remain involved during the evaluation process by providing all needed details. With this approach, customers are more likely to trust the data.

When Phillips Lighting developed its Alto series of mercury-free fluorescent lamps, it knew that existing mercury lamps were toxic and had relatively high disposal costs. Phillips Lighting developed an ROI calculation for its sales team that compared the total cost of ownership for its mercury-free lamps versus competitive lamps. The salespeople changed their normal calling pattern and began working with CFOs at target customers to talk about the financial and environmental benefits of their new product. Alto was not only highly profitable but also won 25 percent of the very price-competitive commercial fluorescent market within two years of the product's introduction.

If customers cannot get comparative data directly from potential suppliers, they will develop their own internal models to facilitate comparison. Once they have done so, it is unlikely that they will

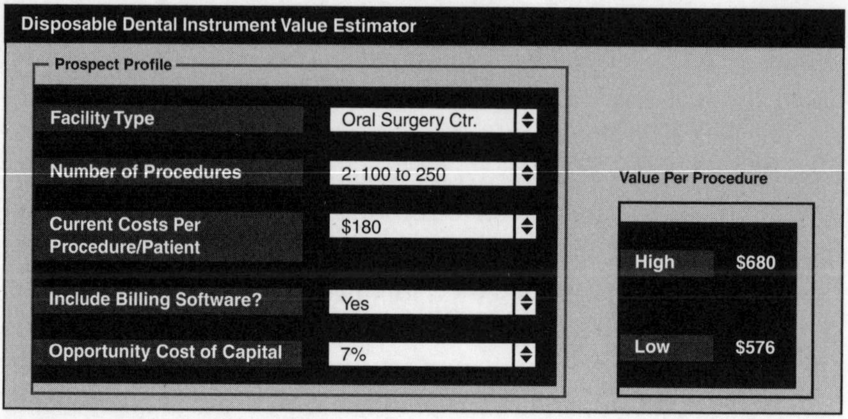

Figure 2.12   Customer Value Insights Drive Credible Sales Tools.

ever share the full details of their analysis. Instead they will use the information to pit one vendor against the other in a game of price negotiation.

Credible sales tools are relatively easy to construct. Going back to our supplier of dental instruments, it is easy to see how the data gathered during conversations with customers can be converted into a compelling sales tool. Notice how simple it is to determine and use a real customer's financial benefit (see Figure 2.12).

Better Value Propositions and Customer Targeting

Often, one of the objectives of this process is to identify customer *triggers* of value. These are operational or profit-model characteristics that allow salespeople to more readily qualify customer needs through simple questioning techniques. These triggers can be based on how a business is operated, what its central strategy is, or a host of other possible things. Once these triggers of value are understood, they can be reduced to a short list of questions that help identify high-value prospects. The key is that the questions must be clear, direct, and result in concrete answers.

We worked with one company that was providing a service to better manage printed marketing materials. The company built its business around increasing efficiency and reducing waste in the development, management, and distribution of such materials. In talking to customers about value, they found that they could reduce customer literature costs by 20 to 40 percent in the first 12 to 18 months of a contract. One of the qualifying questions to target customers may seem surprising: "How much dust is on your catalogs?" If printed catalogs in the storage room had a layer of dust, it was a pretty good indication that the customer had printed too many catalogs or their distribution wasn't well managed.

Once our client identified customers that overinvested in catalog pages that were literally gathering dust, it used its knowledge of customer value to present a clear, quantifiable, and relevant value proposition. "We can reduce the costs of your marketing literature programs by 20 to 40 percent within 12 to 18 months." Due to its efforts in researching customer value, it was able to back up this claim with case studies and customer testimonials. Next, it was able to make a simple statement about how it would achieve these dramatic results. "We are able to reduce your costs by reducing obsolete inventory and by using our technologies to better match supply with your actual literature needs." Finally, it had a compelling first step that allowed it to prove its value to their customers. "To show you what we can do for your business, we'd like to start with an assessment of your current approach to using and managing marketing literature. We will provide a road map for significant improvements in the costs and effectiveness of your current processes and programs."

Think about what this business did. First, it went out and spoke to a few customers to get their input on how they perceived value. It didn't do any fancy market research; it just asked some simple questions. Here are two of the actual questions:

1. "By using our service, did you see improvements in the management of your printed marketing materials?"
2. "If so, what were those improvements and what was their impact?"

From these questions, the company developed a compact and compelling value position with customers. With these powerful tools, the business grew at a rate of 20 percent per year the next two years.

Market research alone can't drive the priorities of the firm. The results need to be linked to a strong sense of understanding of the host of other factors that impact the strategies of the firm. The good news is that the process, once established, is simple and insightful. Also, it's a process that salespeople can understand and work with. That makes them much more likely to implement it. With a small amount of training, your salespeople will gain much more confidence in your pricing and pass it along to your customers.

RULE THREE

APPLY ONE OF THREE SIMPLE PRICING STRATEGIES

Some customers are motivated by price alone. Others want, and are willing to pay for, value. Adjust your offering and selling approach to optimize your advantage for each.

The very idea of a *pricing strategy* makes even the most capable managers nervous. One of our clients put the objection succinctly. "Given the dynamics of today's business environment, how is it possible to settle on a specific pricing strategy without limiting our ability to respond to what's happening in our markets? After all, markets move fast, customer needs change, and our competitors certainly aren't sitting still." Does this song sound familiar? The subtext is clear. We need to move fast. Isn't a pricing strategy too inflexible to do much more than get in the way?

Let's answer the client's question by posing another. If you don't have a well-defined pricing strategy, then who, specifically, is setting your prices? Let's look at the usual suspects. Many companies would say that their customers set prices. But we don't agree. When customers negotiate price, what is their point of leverage? It's your fear that if you don't respond, you will lose the business. It always stings to lose business. But what really motivates companies is a two-headed fear monster: fear that they will lose the business and fear that they will lose the business to a competitor. In that case, not only do they lose but their competitor wins.

Customers are well aware of this fear, skillfully setting up competitors against each other. As a result, companies often make their own pricing decisions based on the perceived pricing strategies of their competitors. So, to the question of who, specifically, is setting your prices, the answer, unfortunately in too many cases, is clear. Your competition is setting your prices for you.

To break this cycle and take back control of pricing, companies must establish a well-reasoned pricing strategy. Intellectually this is not a complicated exercise. A pricing strategy is fairly simple to develop. There are only three choices: skim, neutral, and penetration. Understanding just a few pieces of information can lead you to the right choice. The trick comes in relating your business conditions and objectives to an appropriate pricing strategy. The real challenge is that everyone in the organization has to agree to it.

Here's what happens when everyone is not on the same page. In 2001 DaimlerChrysler replaced the CEO of its Freightliner heavy truck division. Freightliner's use of guaranteed buy-backs on the new trucks it sold flooded the market with used trucks and led to a loss of nearly $500 million. Shortly after taking over, new CEO Rainer Schmuckle announced a number of steps to stabilize pricing, including major revisions to the buy-back program.[1] When called for a response by a reporter, an investor relations executive at one competitor commented that he couldn't envision an end to the price competition that was endemic in the industry. A few weeks later the CEO of the same competitor gave a speech at a major industry conference. The purpose was to try to reverse the damage done by his investor relations team. But it was too late, and a golden opportunity to improve pricing in a brutally competitive industry was missed. Unfortunately, as their results showed, ingrained behaviors made it very difficult to change pricing strategies. In fact the industry continued to have ups and downs until 2006 when macroeconomic conditions led to tightening of supply and upward pricing pressures.

Getting a concensus is important. But once you do, the next step is to be ready to change the strategy. What works in one set of market conditions will fail in another. Pricing strategies must be changed to match market and business conditions. As we will show, you cannot and should not improvise your pricing strategy. Instead there are a small number of variables that can successfully lead to the right strategy, no matter what the market conditions are. In Rule Three, we describe how to identify which pricing strategies will, and will not, work under which conditions. We'll also help you recognize when it's time to change your strategy. Finally, we'll delve into the challenge of organizational alignment.

The Three Basic Pricing Strategies

The three basic pricing strategies are skim, neutral, and penetration. In a skimming strategy, prices are set high relative to mainstream competitors. Use this strategy to maximize revenues generated from the high end of the market. In a neutral pricing strategy, prices are set close to those of your main competitors. Neutral pricing strategies are an important tool when you want to take the focus off of price such as a product in a mature market or in a later stage of its life cycle. Finally, companies that use a penetration pricing strategy set prices quite low relative to the competition. Their objective is to make price a driving factor in the purchase decision. Let's look at each strategy in a little more detail.

Skim Pricing

An essential precondition for *skim pricing* is an offering that customers believe is clearly differentiated from the competition. In general, this means that skim pricing hinges on your ability to demonstrate that your offering provides significantly greater financial benefits than the competition. This occurs in the introductory phase of the product life cycle with early adopters who are generally price insensitive because they see the potential benefits of being the first to deploy a new technology. Since products move through life cycles (more on this later), the only sustainable basis for skim pricing then is the level of differentiation or added value created by the offering. If the level of differentiation declines as more competitors enter the market and match your offering, skim pricing is no longer appropriate since it will price you too high for comparable offerings in the market.

Although skim pricing might seem like the ultimate objective, when used in isolation it is a dangerous tool. Stubbornly sticking to skim pricing creates market opportunities for new competitors. History is littered with the wreckage of market leaders who carved out a position based on highly differentiated offerings and then left room at the low end of the market for second-tier competitors who ultimately unseated the leaders through a focus on moving into higher-value markets. The usual approach for entering second-tier competitors is to first go after more price-sensitive customers that are looking for alternatives to your high-value, high-priced offerings. Once upstart competitors have established market position, they then go after your bread-and-butter customers.

Firms that stick exclusively to skim pricing and premium products do so at their own peril. In the late 1970s Canon decided to take on Xerox in the U.S. copier market. Canon entered the market by recruiting suppliers that could help it build low-cost, low-end compact products. Xerox was slow to respond to this new threat and quickly lost its market-leading position. In addition to being the worldwide market share leader, Canon has continuously racked up impressive results. For close to 20 years in a row, Canon has been the overall market brand leader in the U.S. color laser copier market. Xerox could have prevented its loss of market share by developing a lower value and lower-priced copier perhaps 10 years earlier than they did.

Neutral Pricing

With a *neutral pricing* strategy, prices are set close to the competition with the intention of reducing the impact of price competition. Companies that use neutral pricing typically do so because they want the basis of competition for customer business to be something other than price. They understand that they can't survive a price war. This is often the strategy of choice for second-tier competitors that must carefully compete against a strong market leader. In most cases a neutral pricing strategy is also the best choice when markets are growing slowly or not at all. In these conditions, lower prices are easily matched by competitors and the net effect of price cuts is to decrease margins and the value of the market for all competitors.

Panametrics-NDT (now a part of Olympus Corporation) was a niche marketer of laboratory ultrasound equipment for testing materials' properties when it decided to enter the much larger market for field-portable equipment. The challenge was that this market was dominated by a small number of powerful players that had significantly greater financial resources and extensive customer relationships. The basis for Panametrics' success was technical innovations that were carefully priced just above targeted competitive offerings. Once the firm gained credibility with their top-of-the-line offerings, it introduced a series of additional models: some for the low end of the market and others targeted at specific applications. In each case, the company performed a careful analysis of competitor pricing to ensure that prices on the new models were set in such a way that customers focused on technology and not price differences. While competitors responded with new technology of their own, Panametrics' success in using neutral pricing strategy limited the competitors' ability and likelihood to respond.

Penetration Pricing

Companies use *penetration pricing* strategies precisely because they want price to be the primary driver of the purchase decision. Penetration pricing works when it can be used to establish a dominant market position as Dell did in the 1990s. But, as Dell found out in 2006 and 2007, penetration pricing is also the most misunderstood and abused of all pricing strategies. Time after time managers drop prices in a bid to gain market share. The problem is that price cuts are easy for competitors to match. When they do, no competitor sees an increase in either sales or share.

Penetration pricing causes problems for several reasons. First, the customers who come to you on price are going to be the first to leave when another low-price competitor comes along. Price-based competition, therefore, provides the least sustainable competitive advantage. Second, unless you clearly have a technological edge, chances are someone is going to come along that is a bit better at running their business, has a better operations model, or is more desperate. Just ask the Japanese. They learned this lesson the hard way in a bunch of consumer and high-technology businesses when Korean and now Chinese competitors beat them with lower costs and lower prices.

Many managers also have the mistaken view that low-cost icons such as Dell Computer or Southwest Airlines built their cost positions first and then dropped prices to undercut competition. The reverse is true. Dell and Southwest achieved their positions by relentlessly focusing on the needs of well-defined customer segments and then using this focus to drive costs and prices down to preempt competition.

Confusion about this critical sequence (value first, prices second) leads many companies to mistakenly believe they can use penetration pricing to grab share, achieve economies of scale, and thus create a preferential low-cost position. If it were that easy, everybody would be doing it. Penetration pricing is not that easy. The only condition under which it provides sustainable advantage is when you can preemptively build capacity and use that capacity faster than competitors. Anticipating an increase in industry volume and being the first to expand and take additional volume can preempt capacity investments by competitors because they are left with too little volume or only low-priced business to serve. This is a strategy that must be perfectly executed, otherwise competitors can easily match any attempts to drive major share changes through their own use of penetration pricing. This is happening right now in the flat panel television business.

How to Choose a Pricing Strategy

While relatively simple, choosing a pricing strategy is a high-stakes decision. Choose wisely, and improved pricing performance becomes an engine of organic growth that drives both revenue and profits. Make the wrong decision, and you can start a price war that sucks profits out of the entire industry. Fortunately, there are a number of key indicators that can point you in the right direction.

There are five primary drivers in choosing the right pricing strategy.

1. *The value of your offering relative to the competition:* As we pointed out earlier, your pricing strategy is defined by how you set price levels relative to value.
2. *An understanding of where the offering is in the life cycle:* This is critical because market-level price elasticity changes with each phase of the life cycle. As a result, the best pricing strategy for one phase is often disastrous for another.
3. *Industry economics:* Knowledge of the overall health of your industry (Is utilization increasing or decreasing? What about margins?) and your cost structure is essential. Industries with high fixed costs need to look at pricing strategy differently than industries with high variable costs. Cost structure will also affect how competitors play the pricing game.
4. *Competitive dynamics:* Unless you include competitors' likelihood of responding to your pricing strategy, you are missing a critical element. An analysis of the likelihood that they will accommodate or disrupt your strategy helps define how conservative or aggressive you can be in your approach.

5. *Consensus:* If your organization doesn't have the ability to establish consensus on pricing strategy execution will be a nightmare as different managers adopt very different strategies. To be successful executives and managers need to understand the strategy and what they have to do to execute it successfully.

Value relative to the competition and position in product life cycle serves to define the first cut for considering your pricing strategy options. Depending on the characteristics of your business, your final choice will have to be reconciled with some other key influencers. These include your cost position relative to the competition, how competitors play the competitive game, and industry economic factors such as forward capacity . Let's look at how all of these factors come together to enable the pricing strategy decision.

The Role of Value in Pricing Strategy

If you have high-value, highly differentiated offerings, all pricing strategies are open to you. Hopefully some of your offerings hold this enviable position. Others, invariably, do not. How do you handle the pricing if your offerings don't have a high-value position? Maintaining differentiation in competitive markets for any length of time is brutally difficult. So what do you do when your competitive position changes? Similar to making changes in strategy through the life cycle, you need to be prepared to change your pricing strategy. What can you do when you are at parity with the competition or have fallen behind? While these are uncomfortable positions to be in, there is still money to be made if you choose the right pricing strategy.

There are a number of possibilities to consider. First, what is your best response if your offering is undifferentiated relative to the competition? The answer depends on who is perceived to be the market leader. If you are a market leader and market share is concentrated with a few companies, there is an opportunity to take pricing leadership with a neutral-positive strategy (price slightly higher than the competition) that creates an umbrella for all players. If market share is more dispersed and/or there is no clear market leader, then a neutral strategy is preferred.

If you have a strong value story but the market is dominated by another company that can use its pricing power to drive industry price levels downward (think Intel versus AMD), then respect the power of the market leader and pursue a neutral-negative strategy that is pegged close to, but just below, the market leader's prices.

Another possibility is that your offering is substantially weaker than the competition. There is no reason to despair. As we saw with Canon's success in penetrating the copier market, there are always opportunities to topple market leaders by starting with low-value, low-price products. The key here is to be fearlessly honest about your short-term prospects. It is futile to pretend that your offering's weaknesses will be overlooked. The best response is to use a penetration or neutral-negative strategy as part of an overall plan to penetrate segments of the market that are more price sensitive or not well-served by competitors.

Pricing through the Product Life Cycle

Most products have a finite life cycle. As markets move through their phases of growth and adoption, price strategies have to change, too. Throughout that life cycle there are four distinct stages. The *introductory phase* is marked by slow sales growth as customers learn about the benefits of the new offering. During *growth* customers begin to adopt the offering in increasing numbers and the entrance of new competitors helps speed adoption. During this stage, sales volumes can grow at a breathtaking rate. As products achieve adoption by most potential customers, they enter *maturity*. During this phase, overall market growth slows and begins to level off. Finally, in the *decline* phase, sales volumes drop off as customers move on to other more up-to-date products and technologies.

Overall market response to price (elasticity) is not the same in each stage of the life cycle. The most important thing to understand is that markets are only elastic during one phase: growth. As Figure 3.1 shows, the growth stage is unique in that the rate of growth is high. During the growth phase, customer adoption accelerates as new technologies start to gain broader acceptance. New competitors, seeing the opportunity, also jump in. Ironically, greater competition actually serves to increase the size of the market as more conservative customers perceive that a new technology is a safe bet as it has become more widely available. Increasing customer adoption and the increased visibility brought by new players in the market often combine to accelerate growth. Let's see why this is important and what causes it.

Elastic markets are quite responsive to changes in price. Inelastic markets are not. Understanding price elasticity should inform us when price decreases are going to bring us more revenue such as in elastic markets. And when they are going to bring us less revenue such as in inelastic markets. Simple? Not really, for the following three primary reasons in a BTB environment.

The first reason is that demand in BTB markets is *derived* from some downstream market. This means that demand for your products is not going to be responsive to price changes; it's going to be responsive to

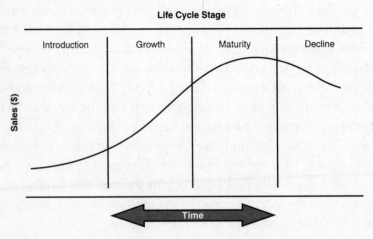

Figure 3.1   Stages in the Product Life Cycle.

how the demand in the downstream market (the customers' demands) changes. As an example, General Electric sells headlights to General Motors. Demand for the headlight bulbs is *derived* by demand for GM automobiles. Any price changes in GE bulbs are unlikely to impact that demand. This makes it, by definition, inelastic. Demand at both the customer level and, generally, at the industry level is going to be inelastic.

The second reason comes down to customer behavior. Some customers will change suppliers often. They don't change their volumes, something that elasticity research tries to capture. They change their suppliers, often due to price. We call that *cross-elasticity of demand*. If we measure cross-elasticity of demand, we can determine a market's responsiveness to our changes in price, but it is unlikely that the volumes will change. That's because of the derived demand. This means that the elasticity we see isn't going to bring more volume into the market.

Finally, you need to include competitive behavior in the mix. Unless you include competitors' willingness to respond and likelihood of responding, you are missing the most important element of the mix. Even if a market is elastic (see Figure 3.2), when a competitor matches your price decrease, they negate any market effect. If your market is inelastic, as most markets are, you've just burned through profits playing a game that you can't win. Let's summarize how this should impact your decision on pricing strategy.

The only stage of the life cycle when markets are elastic is during growth. As Figure 3.2 shows, during all other phases of the product

	Elastic Market	Inelastic Market
Increase Price	Revenue Decreases	Revenue Increases
Decrease Price	Revenue Increases	Revenue Decreases

Figure 3.2   Revenue Impact of Price Changes in Different Market Conditions.

life cycle, decreasing prices will lead to long-run decreases in revenue. You may get a short high from a price cut as customers switch their business to you, but the benefits are short-lived. Competitors will simply match your prices.

Introductory Markets

The pressure to cut prices can be intense. When rolling out an innovative product or service, marketers are focused on identifying and converting *innovators* and *early adopters*. These are customers that actively seek out new and innovative offerings before others do. These customers are desirable for two reasons.

First, they become references for other customers. Second, they provide critical input that translates into market success later in the life cycle. Given these two very significant benefits, companies are often tempted to buy early business with low prices. This temptation is not necessary because their motivations run the gamut from the logical (exploiting the latest technologies to get ahead of the competition) to the emotional (a desire to simply be the first to use an innovation). The decision to be an early adopter is also driven by a desire to advance the company's brand as an innovator operating on the cutting edge of its industry. Regardless of the specific motivation, early adopters are more interested in putting innovation to work than they are in price.

In his groundbreaking work *Diffusion of Innovations*, Everett Rogers estimated that innovators and early adopters make up approximately 16 percent of those that ultimately adopt a technology.[2] Given the limited pool of customers and their relative lack of price sensitivity, the best approach at the introductory phase of the life cycle is to pursue a skimming strategy. Such a strategy has some significant benefits. A high initial price sets the reference for future generations of customers and revisions of the product. Also, a skimming strategy at introduction can actually improve adoption, as early customers will use price as a proxy for value.

There are two major challenges at the introduction phase of a life cycle. The first is selecting the right customers. These are customers who are more likely to accept the risk associated with a new in-novation in order to gain a competitive advantage. If salespeople target the wrong customers, chances are they will all ask for lower prices. Here, the price isn't wrong; the customer is. The second is in proving the value of the innovation. Companies that successfully gain adoption of their innovations do a lot of work to show their value to would-be customers. Failure to address this issue will put the focus back on price as customers decide whether the opportu-nity to determine the value of an innovation is worth the price and associated costs.

To address these thorny issues, marketers need to be aware of what drives adoption of new technologies and use this knowledge to not only drive sales but also to support pricing. Analysis of what drives adoption of new technologies can point marketers in the right direction. Key drivers include:

- Perceptions of compelling advantages over existing technology.
- The ability to observe and measure the impact of those advantages.
- The complexity of the new solution.
- Compatibility with existing processes and technologies.
- The ability to try out an innovation before making a full commitment.

Note that price is not on the list. The list represents a spectrum of what the customer desires to know to mitigate the risks inherent in adopting an innovative new technology. Too often, firms fail to take these drivers of adoption into account when launching an innovative new offering. Instead, the approach is "Our new offering is so innovative that it's hard to prove value or understand risk until we get it into customers' hands. Once they have it, they'll see the genius of what we have created."

The consequence of this assumption is that absurdly low intro-ductory pricing is required to get customers to understand the value of the new offering. But low introductory pricing does more harm than good. First, it results in a lot of money left on the table. Low prices also compound customer perceptions of risk. Under these conditions, customers may reasonably conclude that the low prices factor in some undetected risks, limitations, or seller's desperation.

To avoid this trap, firms need to address the drivers of adoption, point by point, in their launch programs. Consider the case of Azul Systems. This Mountain View, California–based company manufactures server appliances that deliver computer and memory resources as a shared network service. Some years ago, Azul had the audacity to sell one of its early products for an eye-popping $799,000. This product, by the way, was not intended to replace systems provided by competitors. It represented a new platform and new value. Sounds like a hard sell? In fact, the product enjoyed a successful launch because Azul developed a launch program that specifically addressed the major drivers of innovation adoption. Here's how Azul Systems did it.

Azul Systems offered customers an *Economic Advantage Program*, a no-extra-cost private consulting engagement that helps customers quantify the financial gains their organization will realize through a computer pool deployment.

- *Easy Integration:* Integration of Azul's technology requires changing one line of code.
- *Partnership:* Each customer benefited from an Azul-IBM partnership to provide global support, services, spare parts, and training.
- *Certification:* Azul products are certified to work with most major computing hardware and software platforms.
- *Low Risk:* Azul offered a no-cost, 45-day evaluation program for qualified accounts.

Growth Markets

During the growth phase of the life cycle, the number of customers increases dramatically. In addition, many of these customers are relatively inexperienced. These customers will need additional services and support. Existing customers typically begin to expand their usage to peripheral parts of the offering. Given these predictable forces, it makes sense to create bundles of service and support for inexperienced customers. Innovation-driven companies also respond to the increasingly sophisticated needs of their early customers with complementary product and service offerings. They evolve their offerings to meet the differing needs of both high- and low-value segments.

Since a new technology is still unique during the growth phase and given the need to bundle services, a skim-pricing strategy would seem to make sense. There is one major complication. A skim-pricing strategy may retard market growth or open up markets to competitors just as growth begins to accelerate. Sticking with a skim-pricing strategy too long gives these competitors a chance to enter the market with competitive technologies at lower prices. Remember that markets in the growth phase are elastic. This means that lower prices will increase demand and revenues. The key question is how to manage this. Simply lowering prices on your high-value offerings to meet the new competition may help with market share, but it will kill profits in high-end segments. The solution? You need to be the first to *break for the bottom* by lowering prices with a stripped-down offering to flank the high-value offering.

This is exactly what happened to Samsung's cell phone business in China and India in 2006. Samsung maintained a strong focus on the high end of the market as it had successfully done in other markets. The problem was that in these markets, the largest segment of customers can't afford high-end phones. Nokia and Motorola, on the other hand, introduced a sub-$50 handset for these markets and took significant market share. Samsung responded by increasing the number of low-priced handsets for these markets. In an interview in the *Wall Street Journal*, Samsung executive Lee Ki Tae showed his understanding of how to best manage the competitive threat. "If we were to cut our average selling prices now, we could easily reach 20 percent market share, but I'm sure that would be the right move," he said.[3] At the time of the interview Samsung's average handset selling price was $175, compared with Motorola's $131 and Nokia's $124. And the move paid off. In the quarter after this announcement, Samsung's shipments in Asia rose by 28 percent on a sequential basis.

Samsung also achieved its highest market share since the second quarter of 2005.

As an innovation becomes accepted, dropping prices will help accelerate the growth of the market by providing a low-cost means for customers to try it. Also, it provides a low-risk way for more conservative customers to adopt your innovation. These low-risk, low-price customers then serve as a ready pool of candidates to up-sell additional products and services. Finally the break for the bottom enables early market leaders to preempt competition that will come from the low-priced competitors that enter as the market grows. Increasing volumes may drive down costs, thus increasing the ability to control how profitable low-price entrants can become.

Intel deployed the same strategy against Advanced Micro De-vices (AMD). Using its technological lead, Intel would skim price major new products and then drop prices significantly after the vol-ume from early adopters showed signs of leveling off. Doing so not only increased demand but it limited AMD's ability to make suf-ficient margins as it responded with comparable technology. And once customers had chosen Intel microprocessors, they more often purchased additional chip sets based on Intel-provided reference de-signs. AMD wasn't able to break this cycle until they leapfrogged Intel's technology with their Opteron and Athlon 64-bit processors. With these products, AMD dramatically increased profits and saw their market share rise to historic levels.

Mature Markets

As a market moves into maturity, overall demand levels off and the magic of using low prices to grow the whole industry disappears. In fact, because of the effects of derived demand—remember, lower prices don't increase total demand—penetration pricing is poison if you are competing in a mature market. That's because it will actually reduce revenue and cause profits to dramatically decline. Also, penetration pricing increases the likelihood of a price war as competitors will quickly match your price cuts to recover lost market share.

What to do? The best response is to skim price for high margins at the top of the market and use a neutral pricing strategy for mainstream and low-end market segments. Given the need to play the pricing game at multiple levels, it's in mature markets where product managers really earn their keep. After all, the key to making multiple strategies work is a set of offerings that enable you to be successful at all levels of the market.

As markets mature, customer needs become more diverse. Some customers still want, and will pay for, a complete solution: the skim-priced tier of the offering. Others have become quite sophisticated in their knowledge and use of your products and services. These customers are relatively self-sufficient and want only a low-priced, bare-bones offering. Then there are the mainstream customers who have relatively common needs. These customers are where the volume and greatest competition are. Accordingly, a competitive mid-range offering that is priced using a neutral strategy is the way to go here.

Companies that fail to recognize the transition to maturity in their industry typically don't have the offering structure to support this multipronged pricing strategy. They are still in love with the technology and focus on full-featured offerings. When market maturity hits, they have a value mismatch between what they are selling and what customers want to buy. Since they don't have the means to unbundle, the only way they can make up for this mismatch is by discounting prices on a deal-by-deal basis. Results are not guaranteed except in one area. Profits will invariably be devastated.

In addition to manufacturing a range of high-performance, heavy-duty engines for trucks and buses, Caterpillar also offers re-manufactured engines for price-sensitive customers. The company actively promotes this low-end offering and explains why customers might want to consider it. Customers are told that Caterpillar reman-ufactured parts carry a "same as new" warranty to assure worry-free ownership. Price-sensitive customers benefit from remanufactured products that cost 20 to 60 percent less than new products. The company benefits by having a lower-priced flanking offering for customers who resist the prices of new products. These customers remain Caterpillar customers by not defecting to the competition and may be in a position to pay higher prices for new products in the future.

There is one exception to this rule. If you are in the enviable position of being a cost leader, then all bets are off. Cost leadership brings with it some substantial and unique rewards that lead to different decisions around pricing strategy. Often, cost leaders enter markets not by taking on the leaders but rather by serving the most price-sensitive customers first. For them, penetration pricing is the strategy of choice. This approach is typically sustainable through the growth and possibly early maturity phases of the product life cycle. As the market moves deeper into maturity, even cost leaders need to consider adding enhanced offerings and higher-end products to reap profits from niche segments that begin to appear.

Failure to understand this transition cost Dell Computer its market leadership position in 2006. In response to the threat of a newly revitalized Hewlett-Packard, Dell aggressively dropped prices to win market share. The result? Profits dropped 51 percent from the prior year. Commenting on their problems in a *New York Times* interview on August 18, 2006, Michael Dell and Kevin Rollins noted, "We cut prices too aggressively in a number of markets to win market share. We didn't do a good job of it at all." An increase in PC sales of 6 percent translated into an operating profit *decline* of 48 percent.

At the time, Gartner research reported that PC unit sales were projected to grow 10 percent, but revenue was going to decline 2.5 percent. Read that as mature and/or declining market. When you use lower prices expecting demand to follow, it doesn't work, because competitors match the price. Dell kept using price as a competitive weapon and saw profits crash. On the other side, Hewlett-Packard got its costs under control and began to win customers based on superior features. They introduced more appealing computers that were available in a broad range of consumer outlets. People can drop by a retail store and get their machines in 30 minutes, rather than four days. And, they get to play with them first.

This double whammy caused Dell to revamp its strategy. Dell dropped its focus on market share and even reached agreement to start selling their PCs through Wal-Mart. Early on in this process, things started to improve. In November 2006, Dell reported increased sales of only 6 percent, with total company growth of just 3.4 percent. However, the company reported net income growth of 30 percent. Dell publicly changed its pricing strategy, refusing to compete on price. Dell was also more selective in its battle for corporate relationships. The net result was that they traded a drop in PC market share of about 1 percent in return for gross margin improvement from 15 percent to over 17 percent.

Declining Markets

In declining markets, diminishing demand is sustained by customers that have a strong preference for a particular technology. This preference is typically strong enough to make declining markets relatively price insensitive. In the nineteenth century, there were hundreds of buggy whip manufacturers in America. We are sure that the last buggy whip manufacturer in business made a wonderful product for customers who were happy to pay whatever the company asked. For this company, the best move was to focus exclusively on a skim-pricing strategy.

To understand how this works, let's look at the market for another technology that many people think is dead, but surprisingly is doing quite well: vacuum tubes. The forerunners of today's integrated circuits were once very common, powering every radio and television set. Today, vacuum tubes are still popular among audio enthusiasts and musicians who value the warm sound qualities they are thought to deliver. These loyal customers are willing to pay for that performance. Consider a commonly used preamplifier tube. A typical price for vacuum tubes is $10 to $20. By contrast, an integrated circuit that performs the exact same functions with greater

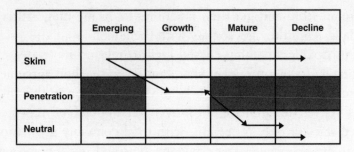

Figure 3.3   Avoid the "Red Zones" by Changing Pricing Strategy throughout the Life Cycle.

control and reliability costs pennies. In a similar vein, despite the fact that it is a declining market, IBM continues to reap the rewards of being one of the few providers of mainframe computers, despite having received advice in the 1990s to leave that business because it was in decline.

Be Prepared to Change

The key to successful pricing strategy over a product's life cycle is your readiness to change. Remember, what works in one phase won't in the next. Since most offerings spend the greatest percentage of their time on the market in either the growth or maturity phases of the life cycle, you need to be able to simultaneously manage multiple strategies. As we've already discussed, the key to this is actually your offering strategy. By focusing on the concepts of derived demand and price elasticity, you can arrive at a basic strategy that will produce healthy revenues and profits no matter what stage of the life cycle your offering is in. Figure 3.3 illustrates what strategies are called for in different phases of the life cycle.

Pricing Strategy for Capital-Intensive Businesses

For companies with investments in plant and equipment, you need to consider overall industry capacity and capacity utilization when selecting pricing strategy. In times of excess capacity, it makes sense to adjust prices downward only to the extent that the price cut helps utilize plant capacity. Capacity share and market share tend to equalize over time. Attempts to increase share during times of excess capacity through use of a penetration pricing strategy can be easily matched and negated by competition.

Conversely, as capacity begins to become scarce, it makes sense to start bringing overall price levels up. Failure to do so leaves a company vulnerable to having to fill capacity with low-priced business. The potential damage can be actually worse if smart competitors start shedding their most price-sensitive customers with the intention of foisting them on you. The end result will be a sharp decline in your company's profits.

In the final stage of the business, when the industry is operating at or near capacity, the safe decision is to pursue a skimming strategy. There is just one caveat. Always treat loyal customers fairly. While in theory you may be able to extract more profit from them at the top of the cycle, they will resent having their loyalty betrayed. Long-term customer relationships are valuable. To the extent customers consider your company as a partner, they will resist taking advantage when your company is at the bottom of the cycle. While this will mean forgone profits during good times, it will also mean more stable profits during slow times when the business of loyal customers is more meaningful. We discuss this more in Rule Five, "Price to Increase Profits."

Pricing Strategy for Businesses with High Up-Front Costs

For businesses with high development but low production costs such as providers of software and information products, a different set of economic issues drives pricing strategy decisions. As Carl Shapiro and Hal Varian point out in their groundbreaking article "Versioning: The Smart Way to Sell Information," information goods (goods that can be distributed in a digital form) have always been characterized by a distinct cost structure. "Producing the first copy is often very expensive, but producing subsequent copies is very cheap," they write, adding that the fixed costs for information products are most often sunk.[4] In other words, the cost of producing that first copy often cannot quickly be recovered, while the variable costs of producing each incremental copy often do not change even with significant increases in volume. As such, producers of information products have very few, if any, capacity constraints.

What are the implications of this unique cost structure for pricing strategy? The principal difference comes during the early stages of the life cycle. Here providers of information products have to address two fundamental questions. The first question: "Is the market that we are entering going to be driven by standards?" The second: "If the market is standards-driven, will customers move quickly to award leadership in our product category?" If the answer to both of these questions is "Yes," then the best move is to adopt a penetration pricing strategy from the very start.

With traditional products and services, the best approach is to stake a strong position at the high-value end of the market supported by skim or neutral-positive pricing strategies and work down-market to protect your flanks. In contrast, information products companies typically have to turn this approach upside-down. The best approach is often to view the low-value, penetration priced offering as the engine of growth supported by a gradual move toward the high-value, more complex services as customers become more sophisticated. In addition to increasing your chances at winning the standards game, this approach addresses another unique characteristic of information goods in that they are *experience* products whose quality is uncertain until the customer gets to try them out.

EDGAR Online has built a business around enhancing data and reports that are provided free-of-charge via the SEC's EDGAR (Electronic Data Gathering Analysis and Retrieval) database. So how do you build a business around public information that is available for free? It starts with the insight that the free version inevitably generates demand for resources to turn the information into knowledge. So while the SEC provides the information without cost, there are very limited capabilities to search, analyze, and manipulate the data.

Users can purchase subscriptions from EDGAR Online that provide subscribers with the advanced capabilities they need. So sure is EDGAR Online of their services, that it provides visitors to Yahoo! Finance and Nasdaq.com with free seven-day trials of their premium offering. Even the SEC benefits in that, to the extent EDGAR Online provides the most desirable analytical capabilities, the agency is spared from developing the services itself. In fact, in their own SEC filings, EDGAR Online specifically credits Nasdaq.com and Yahoo! Finance as the principal sources for new subscriptions.

The Competitive Landscape and Pricing Strategy Options

Ultimately, pricing strategy has to be measured against what the competition is currently doing or is capable of doing. There are two principal issues that pricing managers need to consider. First, what is the firm's cost position relative to the competition? Second, given the different options for an emerging pricing strategy, how is the competition likely to respond?

When looking at potential competitive responses, there are some obvious strategies to avoid. Penetration pricing against a low-cost leader is a nonstarter. The same is true in relying heavily on skim pricing against competition that has a win-at-all-costs–lose-no-deal-on-price mentality. We'll talk more about playing the competitive game in the discussion of Rule Seven, "Force Your Competitor to React to Your Pricing." If you are uncertain about how competitors will respond, here's a helpful hint to avoid destructive price competition. When facing a volatile competitor, a neutral pricing strategy is always the safest. To support your strategy, it always pays to be able to keep competitors worried that you will adopt a penetration strategy if needed to defend your market position. This reduces the likelihood that they will adopt a penetration strategy against you.

Final Thoughts: Be Prepared to Change Your Strategy

It's not really that tough to pick a pricing strategy. The real challenge comes when the market changes and you have to change your strategy quickly. So what are some signs that conditions require a change in pricing strategy? Here are a few to keep an eye on:

- *Unit sales volume growth slows down:* This, along with a change in customer price response, is the primary indicator of a transition from one phase of the life cycle to the next. When entering the growth phase of the market, if you grow but not as fast as the competition. It may be time to lower prices. When moving from growth to maturity, growth starts coming more and more at the expense of the competition. When this happens, it's time to deploy multiple strategies, especially neutral prices.
- *Discounts fail to drive incremental volume:* Look at the graphs of price discounting versus gross sales growth. When one line starts heading up (discounting) and the other starts heading down (sales growth), this is a signal that it's time to start thinking about changing your strategy.
- *Competitors introduce new offerings:* Time to check your value positioning. Have you gone from being a leader to being a laggard? If so, you need to move away from skim-pricing strategies.
- *Lower-cost competitors enter the market:* Are you providing an umbrella for them? Will they come after your high-value customers? If so, you need to move to protect your flanks with a penetration priced offering.
- *Competitors start missing their numbers:* There is nothing more dangerous than a desperate competitor. Time to try to take the focus off of price.

Defining and managing your pricing strategy is straightforward, if you focus on a few simple things. You must understand the true nature of the demand for your offerings, their value, and position in the life cycle. You must understand a little about the economics of your business and how your competitors run theirs. Most managers are aware of these issues. In many cases, they just haven't put together what they already know in a way that helps with pricing strategy. The beauty of it all is that it can be done, and often quite quickly. The result? Increased revenues and profits. Not a bad return for a short amount of time thinking about your business.

Notes

1. Jeffrey Ball, "DaimlerChrysler's Freightliner Pushes to Revise Costly Trucking-Fleet Pacts," *Wall Street Journal*, October 5, 2001.
2. Everett Rogers and Everett M. Rogers (2003). *Diffusion of Innovations, 5th Edition*, New York, NY: The Free Press.
3. Yun-Hee Kim, "Samsung Changes Its Strategy in Bid to Regain Market Share," *Wall Street Journal*, December 6, 2006.
4. Carl Shapiro and Hal A. Varian, "Versioning: The Smart Way to Sell Information," *Harvard Business Review*, November–December 1998, Cambridge, MA.

RULE FOUR

PLAY BETTER POKER
WITH CUSTOMERS

All customers say that value is what they most want, but many are bluffing. Some customers are motivated by price alone. Others want, and are willing to pay for, value. Know the difference, so the difference can work for you. Adjust your offering and selling approach to optimize your advantage for each. You might even learn to love your price buyers. It's the poker players you've got to control.

E
veryone wants value. The reality, however, is that not everyone is willing to pay for it. Customers think differently about value and about vendors. Some customers want great relationships. Some only want to buy at the lowest price. To be successful, salespeople and managers need to recognize those differences and craft the right customer approaches if they don't want to waste their time and leave money on the table.

Customers have different agendas for different vendors. Each agenda and subsequent buyer behavior requires a very different offering, pricing, and selling approach. We have identified four types of customers: price buyers, value buyers, relationship buyers, and a unique group we call poker-playing buyers. Let's introduce the four groups, and then we will examine them at greater length so you can immediately recognize each variation and know how to engage with them.

Price Buyers

These customers buy exclusively on price. They don't care about value-added enhancements, nor do they care about fancy bells and whistles. They establish purchasing criteria for a wide range of possible vendors and make sure they qualify every one to bid on the business. Price buyers are very careful not to let themselves get committed to any particular supplier by making sure they have no switching costs. Perhaps the two best examples of price buyers are General Motors and the U.S. government. Both organizations focus on price, using these tactics to the detriment of many suppliers.

Value Buyers

Some customers are willing to switch from one supplier to another based on their ability to improve their financial picture or impact for their clients. These customers have recognized the flaws of price-only purchasing and often have very sophisticated technical and business process people who regularly evaluate the value that alternative vendors offer. Two of the best examples of value buying are from Toyota and Wal-Mart. Yes, they are at times brutal, but they have a long history of working with and supporting vendors as long as the vendors are willing to continuously improve the cost effectiveness of their two organizations. Toyota and Wal-Mart will often provide technical support to their vendors so they can do that.

Relationship Buyers

These customers rely on close relationships with suppliers. Relationship buyers trust that their vendor partners will provide solutions and services the customers need to win market share against their own competitors. A surprising result of understanding the drivers of relationship buying is that many companies see their customers as being price-oriented yet they actually have customers that want stronger relationships.

In the IT environment where price buying appears to dominate, in truth, only 30 percent of customers "get the relationships they want" and 70 percent said that "they want to move away from purely transactional relationship by establishing stronger partnerships with a smaller number of preferred IT suppliers."[1] Unfortunately, the reason the customers seem like price buyers is because the salespeople are calling on the wrong individuals in the buying companies or because the salespeople cave on price so quickly that customers know they can negotiate. Believe it or not, one of the biggest distinctions that relationship buyers have versus price buyers is their level of trust in their supplier. That's an important distinction since the activities that companies need to do to develop trust are different than many of the relationship building exercises that we see in many sales programs.

Poker-Playing Buyers

Poker players love to play the pricing game. They have learned that if they focus on price, they can often get vendors to leave money on the table and still continue to provide high-value features and services. This often comes in the mature phase of a life cycle when buyers are more sophisticated and are no longer worried about getting access to the product. Poker players know suppliers will do just about anything to get their business.

Distinguishing among and developing sales strategies for four types of buyers is difficult enough. What complicates matters is that most companies overestimate the ratio of price buyers to value and relationship buyers. We did an experiment at one company we visited—a manufacturer of high-value electronic equipment. First we asked the salespeople to estimate the percentage of price buyers among its customers. The salespeople consulted with each other and estimated that 70 percent of their customers were price buyers. Then they did some actual research that determined that only 30 percent of customers were price buyers. The difference was most likely made up of poker players.

How to Identify a Customer's Behavior

It is vital that a company going into negotiations with a customer knows in advance what kind of buyer that customer is. An excellent negotiating approach for one type of buyer will fail with a buyer working on a different paradigm.

Several years ago, we were working with a large paper company. Our primary activity was training managers on strategic pricing skills, but we also did a lot of coaching on selling skills and customer negotiations. We got a call from a senior sales executive who wanted our advice to prepare for a negotiation with a large customer. Her strategy was perfect for a relationship buyer. Unfortunately, we determined that the customer was a price buyer. After discussions, we predicted that her company had very little chance of winning the business from this particular buyer using the indicated strategy. We suggested she change her strategy or use her time to focus on more promising customers. The executive angrily rejected our recommendation and plowed ahead with her team to prepare for the battle. Two weeks later we heard they had lost the deal.

How did we know the buyer in question was a price buyer and not a relationship buyer? The triggers are not hard to detect if you know what to look for. Here are some of the facts and what we heard. First, the selling company was not the low-cost supplier in the business. It did offer the high value-add product in this particular business area. It did have a long-term relationship with the client, but that client had recently been purchased by a conglomerate that had a long history of price buying. Further, we learned that the buyer from the conglomerate had taken over the purchasing of the particular product offered by our client and had invited a number of other companies to submit bids along with our client's. This was clearly a price buying situation. Our client was not equipped to win since they hadn't yet established any low-value flanking products.

The sales executive had unrealistic expectations. She wanted to win the order but didn't have the tools or product offering to do it. To win in the game of customer negotiations, the salesperson must have a clear vision of what it is the customer truly wants, what they're willing to pay, and the ability to subsequently sell it to them. Understanding the likely buying behavior is critical because it tells the seller, first, whether there is a chance of winning the business and, second, what needs to be done to make sure no money is left on the table.

With price buyers, the decision is almost always controlled by a purchasing agent. That purchasing agent will have experience in negotiating and purchasing that particular product. He will qualify quite a few suppliers that can meet the specifications. Those specs define the *commodity solution* in the marketplace. Their approach to dealing with suppliers can be cold and, in extreme cases, can be abusive.

At the opposite end of the spectrum, relationship customers tend to be mid-sized and smaller companies relying on suppliers to give them the skills in the product or service area. Here, the decision is likely driven by someone senior in the organization. For smaller companies, it may even be the president or owner. Their style in dealing with suppliers is very open. They're glad to have trusted partners, and in return will be as helpful to you as possible in defining their needs. Because of their loyalty, they often have only one vendor qualified for a particular area.

Value buyers want clear demonstrable value from suppliers. Accordingly, they have the internal expertise to evaluate that value to the organization or to their clients. The evaluator has technical expertise or specific experience to understand the value differences between different suppliers' offerings. Their style in dealing with vendors is open but somewhat controlling. They want to know what the vendor can offer but also want to control the process. Here, while the buying process may be supported or fronted by a purchasing agent, the real control lies with a department manager or someone on the technical staff, from IT, production, or engineering. Since value buyers need the resources to do this, they are typically mid-sized to larger companies.

Poker players frustrate most suppliers. These are the customers who want the relationship and acknowledge the real value of the offering, but know that if they put the seller up against a bunch of low-value vendors, the price will drop. Perhaps the clearest signal in dealing with a poker player is when the decision is being handled by a third-party consultant or a buyer who is relatively new to the company or the buying team. In either case, their basic premise is "Watch me make your suppliers roll over and cut price." They will often do this with a very well defined RFP. But, you need to watch the vendor list since it often includes providers who do not have the capabilities to meet the requirements of the bid. Such companies are on the list just to put downward pressure on prices.

Watch for Customers Who *Behave* as Price Buyers

Many customers have discovered that they can obtain value without paying for it by *behaving* as if price is the only thing that matters. It is amazing some of the things that poker-playing purchasing agents will do to extract lower prices from vendors. Equally amazing are the number of vendors who train their customers to expect lower prices to make the quarterly goals. An excellent list of some of those poker-playing behaviors is compiled by Larry Steinmetz and Bill Brooks in their book *How to Sell at Margins Higher Than Your Competitors: Winning Every Sale at Full Price, Rate, or Fee.* Following are our favorites from their list. You'll be embarrassed by how many times you or your salespeople have been fooled by a purchasing agent pulling one of these tricks.

Purchasing Agent Tricks to Get You to Cut Your Price

1. They stiff-arm the rep.
2. They imply (or flatly state) that your competitor's quality, service, and delivery is as good or better than yours.
3. They say, "Let's write it up at a lower price this time. We'll see if we can't pay more later when we know how well you perform."
4. They say, "We don't care about quality, service, or delivery. They don't make any difference. Price is all that's important."
5. They assert you have to meet certain requirements, such as, "we can pay only X dollars per unit."
6. They say you can use their name as a reference to other, potential customers.
7. They keep stalling, looking for concessions.
8. They insist that the users—the people out in the shop, in the office or in the field that use your product—don't see any difference in your products from other's products.
9. They do their homework and they know about problems your company is having.
10. They use the old "Rock Bottom Price" ploy.
11. They hit you with terms to their advantage and use false (negotiating) breaking-off points.
12. Sometimes, they'll use a shill to negotiate with you.
13. They ask for throw-ins. This is called *nibbling*.
14. They walk out on the deal occasionally—just to "teach you."
15. They learn to get tougher at the end of the negotiations.
16. They say, "We need to reduce to only two vendors. If you want to be one of them, you will have to cut your price."
17. They say, "I need a reason to cut off this long-term vendor. For me to do so, you must be below their price."
18. They say, "We need a prototype. Let's get samples in here." Or "Let's get some drawings in here. We'll worry about the price then."
19. They play the power game relative to how the furniture is organized, where to sit and even on what to sit.[2]

Salespeople and managers still fall for these tactics even when they know the customer needs value. These same salespeople and sales managers have purchasing agents in their own company who are experts on doing the same thing with *their* suppliers. How hard would it be to take a walk across the office and talk to your own purchasing agents to find out some of the tricks they play with their vendors?

Poker players can be identified by sudden changes in the buying center. That is, a technical manager with high levels of power will suddenly drop from the relationship and a purchasing agent will take over. If that move is preceded by a significant downturn in profits for the customer, it may indicate that the true behavior has moved to price buying. But, if the move seems to come as a total surprise, it may signify the move to poker playing.

Believe it or not, you don't need to worry about whether you've got a real poker player on your hands. If you treat them like a price buyer, you automatically minimize the damage they can inflict on your company and on your profits. Alternatively, you can expose them by pulling something of value out of the solution to meet this price. You will see if they badly need the value item or not. The real trick is to try to understand their real power over the final decision. They may say they have complete control over the decision, but often they don't. They may even try to block your access to other members of the buying center. But if you can talk to them, you can find out what the poker player's real power is.

How to Respond to Each Behavior

We recently had a situation with a prospective client interested in retaining our consulting services. The negotiation involved submitting and refining bids through a number of RFP cycles. Our strategy was to use these RFP cycles to gradually encourage value buying behavior. So at each cycle, our bid did not directly respond to the RFP. Rather, we used the opportunity to present a series of questions to qualify the prospective client and sharpen its thinking about what it wanted to accomplish. We recognized that we could use the RFP cycles to take the prospect to a deeper level of thinking about value and price. We won the project. Terrific. But then, the purchasing agent showed up and tried to extract further price concessions. But we were ready for him. We conceded that, yes, it would be possible to lower the price. Of course, that would mean either reducing the number of research interviews in the scope of work or conducting more over the phone. We told him this would sacrifice the quality and reliability of the results on which the client was about to base a strategic, multimillion-dollar decision. The purchasing agent retreated, revealing the company's true identity as a value buyer. They wanted—and were willing to pay for—the extra value we offered. The purchasing agent eventually signed off on a purchase order for significantly more dollars than we originally quoted.

The first rule in dealing with price buyers is to be very careful of getting into bidding wars with competitors. There are no winners in price wars, only survivors. Price buyers use bidding wars to drive prices down. Winners suffer from the *winner's curse*.[3] That is, they win the order but end up losing so much in margin dollars that they wish they hadn't taken the order. It is unlikely that they'll be able to make it up in volume or over time. That's because as soon as the supplier tries to raise prices, the price buyer switches to another supplier who makes the same mistake. To help protect against being burned by a price war, we recommend establishing a *walk-away price* when dealing with price buyers. Before you enter into negotiations with a price buyer, it is vital that salespeople establish the bottom price based on a good understanding of the current business loading and cost structure. Make sure that this calculation is done back at the office when everyone is thinking about a profitable business rather than fighting over winning an order.

Only offer bare minimum solutions to price buyers. Strip away all extra features and services. These buyers don't want them. Not even if they are free. And never expect they are going to become relationship buyers based on getting the extras. Unless lightning strikes or they have a change in people or strategy, they never will.

Price buyers have no loyalty. They don't want to be loyal. They actually like to switch; it's part of their individual and corporate DNA. They work to prevent sellers from introducing switching costs into the mix. We don't understand why companies expect the basic rules of buyer behavior to change. A few years ago BellSouth was surprised when 35,000 customers who bought its DSL service for a six-month special promotional price of $9.95 per month switched to competitors when the program was over. The competitors offered slightly better terms.

Value buyers are those customers who understand and are willing to pay for value. In fact, these buyers often will turn down a vendor just because they don't offer choices with different ranges of value. When we researched this issue, we found that many value and relationship buyers were disappointed when salespeople didn't know how to present options to them. We advise you to invest in understanding the value buyer's business. Conduct the depth interviews. Do the ROI calculations. Take ownership of the customer's results. Call beyond the purchasing agent to other members of the buying center. When putting together the offering package, make sure it gives them choices, especially when the high-value choice is going to be over budget. Give them an option that meets their budget. And, provide the necessary analysis to help them make the best choice.

We were in a situation with a prospective client that was working with a $50,000 training budget. What they were really asking for was $80,000 worth of work. Rather than just give them the higher-priced bid and probably price ourselves out of the engagement, we gave the prospect two solutions. The first option was for $45,000 and the other was for $80,000. The decision maker felt that we had done our job and, after reflecting on his company's true training needs, decided on the higher-value offering. If we hadn't offered the choice, he would have thought that we were just too expensive.

Value buyers can become loyal. But it may take a while. It is best to start value buyers off with small elements of a solution so they can test and see the value for themselves. The result, over time, is that they begin to trust the capabilities of the vendor and see more benefit to making them part of their overall solution. At this point, the vendor almost always enjoys a favorable consideration in the procurement process. These are wonderful accounts to have because the seller gets profitable revenue for an extended period of time.

Relationship buyers really want to be taken care of. They expect their vendors are going to do the best job possible meeting their needs. They usually rely on their vendors to provide them with the technical expertise to make systems, machines, and processes work. They rely on vendors for training, too. These are the customers that need to connect with the selling organization's senior executives on a regular and planned basis.

Relationship customers expect their vendors to carry a complete line of products and services. And, they are willing to pay for the commitment to inventory and services. The more breadth of items they can get from a single vendor they trust, the more confidence they have. This confidence reduces their cost of purchasing and, more importantly, their risk.

If you have radically new technology to introduce, make it available to value buyers first because they have the internal expertise to accommodate the risk of new technology. Make it available to relationship buyers only when it has become proven or more stable. You basically want to become their expert advisor in your product and technology area. It reduces the relationship buyer's investment and makes their risk lower.

Relationship customers may become loyal to you over time. It is hard to target such customers because they have been historically loyal to a competitive vendor or have an internal department, even if the cost of that department is high or its efficiency is low. If you are going to target a company that is loyal to a competitor or an internal department, an ROI value analysis is a good start. But it will take more than an ROI value analysis to win their allegiance. Low prices are not their hot button—reliability is. So while low prices seem appealing, they generally lead to a response from the competitor and perhaps the start of a price war. It is best to start working slowly with a relationship customer. Look for a small need to fulfill and do it well. Prove your reliability. Identify a problem that their current vendor missed and offer to solve it. Like a value buyer, relationship buyers like to build trust with their vendors.

But do not take advantage of a relationship buyer's dependence on you. Digital Equipment Corporation took advantage of its relationship customers by locking them in through software and service contracts and then charging relentlessly higher prices. When the customers recognized that, they quickly rebelled. Many became poker players, which raised DEC's costs and reduced their margins. Other customers defected to lower-cost computing platforms. Soon DEC faltered and then had to sell the business. Make sure you treat relationship customers fairly if you want them to remain relationship customers.

The solution is to have a dual-services bundling approach that has a low-price, bare-bones offering and a higher-price, full-service offering. This prevents alienation and gives salespeople something of value they can sell to relationship-oriented customers. Offering choices to customers is powerful because it helps the salespeople clearly differentiate why one price is higher than the other. In most markets, there are more value- or relationship-oriented customers than price-oriented customers, and they want choices. It often doesn't seem like that because suppliers do things such as tacking on surcharges that cause customers not to trust them. When that happens, all customers start to act like price buyers.

The Importance of Trust

In dealing with both relationship and value buyers, trust is vital. Research we conducted a number of years ago in the sale of commodity circuit boards to seven different industries found that there were two major drivers of price buying behavior. The first driver was the size of the company. The second was the level of trust in both the selling company and salesperson. That's important because if there isn't a plan to develop trust with customers, they are going to be either price buyers or poker players. Company size makes a big difference, too, because larger companies have the wherewithal to develop the internal expertise they need to evaluate alternative vendors. Because they are resource-rich, they risk leaving money on the table by not buying based on price. For the others, our research identified the following drivers of trust between buyers and sellers:

- Lack of high-pressure selling tactics.
- Supplies quality as promised.
- Responsive customer service.
- Listens to my problems (depth research).
- General company reliability.
- On-time delivery.
- General salesperson reliability.
- Experience of both the salesperson and the buyer.
- Salesperson product expertise.

Even though not the complete list from the research, these items do make a number of important points. First, general reliability of both the salesperson and the supplying company in a number of areas is critical for developing trust. Second, if there is high turnover on the vendor side or if the customer has high turnover on their side, there is going to be more price buying behavior. Finally, investments in salesperson product expertise are well spent. Teach them how to listen and conduct depth interviews to dive into the customer's issues. What's the bottom line? If these things aren't done, all of your customers are going to look like price buyers.

Play Better Poker

The poker player is the hardest customer to deal with. That's because these are the people who want to get high value for low price and are accustomed to getting it. They negotiate for the lowest prices and spend the rest of their time hollering for increased services. If you want to stop leaving money on the table when you are playing with poker players, you simply have to play better poker or not play at all.

There are a number of reasons that customers play poker. One is that they have learned not to trust their vendors. The biggest reason, however, is because experience shows them it works in lowering prices. Most vendors, even big ones in very high-value markets, just don't know how to effectively respond to poker players. There are only three ways to win at poker. Either have a winning hand, bluff, or fold. Most successful poker-playing customers don't want to rely on the luck of the draw, and they generally prefer not to drive away vendors with whom they have a successful relationship. But they are very eager to bluff. This is what many purchasing agents have specialized in over the years. The problem is that salespeople and their managers haven't developed their own set of bluffing skills. Nor do they realize the strength of their own hand. Without the confidence gained from knowing their own power, salespeople and managers lose in customer negotiations because they are desperate to close the deal at any price.

Professional services firms and IT outsourcing companies are prime examples of companies saddled with a high incidence of poker-playing customers. These customers, supported by armies of third-party consultants, have learned to play aggressive poker and to know the finer elements of the bluff. The professional services firms fold on each bluff and give away huge amounts of value and profits through lower prices. In some cases, because these firms customize every solution for every customer, they cannot easily discriminate the different levels of value for their customers.

Wachovia Bank recently integrated its securities division with Prudential Securities. When the IT switch was turned on, nearly one-third of the integrated company's computers went down. As the week wore on, rather than getting better, the situation got worse. We estimated that the minimum loss in revenue was probably more than $30 million. Now let's add the opportunity costs and lost customers from this major technology meltdown—probably another $100 million. Does Wachovia think that professional services are commodities anymore?

Services Are Not a Commodity

Wouldn't you love to see a celebrity poker game with buyers and sellers of professional services? Just imagine who would fill the losers lounge first. It can all be avoided if firms chant a simple mantra: Services are not a commodity. One more time, because this is the reality—Services are not a commodity. Why don't customers tell you that? Because it's not in their best interests to do so. Their negotiating power is much enhanced if you accept their bluff that services are commodities. They're not, and if you call their bluff, nine times out of ten they will fold.

We see evidence that the overall percentage of poker players is increasing. This increase results from the combination of increased sophistication of customers, desperation of competitors, and the collective inability of many salespeople to deal with customer tactics. So, what's a salesperson to do? First, and perhaps most important, treat the poker player like a price buyer. If they want a low price, give it to them, if you possibly can. Again, make sure they get low-value products and services. Also, install solid fences so they can't get access to the higher-value services.

This requires some level of collective courage in the organization. When a poker player wins the negotiation at a low price and then calls to get services that weren't part of the original deal, you've got to say no. Tell other managers and employees that it's okay for them to say no, too, or to ask for an additional purchase order to pay for them.

Do a value- and buying-center analysis at poker player customer organizations. Even if it is based on some guesses and suppositions, such an analysis is the equivalent of estimating the hand of an opposing poker player. Do some homework on the estimated value of your products and services. It's a liberating experience. Knowing how much value your company's products and services are really providing strengthens your hand. Often the poker playing is done by a purchasing agent or third-party consultant who has assured the real decision maker that they're going to win this one. In fact, they probably bragged about it. To win, they're going to be a strong gatekeeper to keep the vendor away from the real influencers and decision makers. The trick here is to do everything possible to get access to the other members of the buying center. Take walks around the customer offices, if possible. Take time to prepare technical and financial questions to get past the buyer to the right people. Go visit with the users or with a technical person to find out what they're doing. We once got past the gatekeeper in poker-playing mode by having a technical person walk in with pizza for the technical staff. He found out everything he needed to by taking time to understand the technological problems the customer was trying to solve. The purchasing agent lost that round.

With poker players, the negotiating planning takes on an additional purpose. Not only does it prepare salespeople for what is coming, it also prepares their senior managers. A common tactic of poker players is to go over the heads of the sales professionals. They know that senior managers are more likely to cave on price in the middle of a negotiation. Part of the account planning process with poker players is to make sure that senior managers agree to a pricing strategy and stick to it.

If you really want to stop leaving money on the table and stop senseless discounting, invest in learning how to play better poker with customers. Rather than hating it, you might even start to enjoy the game. Learn to bluff and learn to get up and walk away from the table when you still hold value in your hand. Then you can begin to close deals confidently and profitably.

Notes

1. Baljit S. Dall and Andrew S. West, "Building Stronger IT Vendor Relationships." *Innovations in IT Management*, No. 4, Spring 2005.
2. Lawrence Steinmetz and William T. Brooks. (2005). *How to Sell at Margins Higher Than Your Competitors: Winning Every Sale at Full Price, Rate, or Fee*, Hoboken, NJ: Wiley.
3. Richard H. Thaler. (1994). *The Winner's Curse*, Princeton, NJ: Princeton University Press.

RULE FIVE

PRICE TO INCREASE PROFITS

It's a myth that if you grow the top line by increasing sales, you will see increased profits. Profits result when an organization does many things right, including pricing. Efficiency, controlling costs, better profit metrics—all are required for pricing success.

M anagers worry too much about revenue and not enough about profits. They count on cost declines in operations to improve profits. Eventually, cost declines level out and profits begin to decline. To make matters worse, costing systems often prevent reductions in price when it might be appropriate. Those costing systems also make the introduction of lower-value flanking products and services look unprofitable when in many cases they can increase profits. Rule Five is about using price to increase profits, but it is also about simplifying costing approaches so they permit more effective use of your company's resources, be they people or machines, to increase both profits and revenue.

Let's start with the basics. The highest purpose for price is to improve profits. This is the purpose that adds profits and, when appropriate, adds revenue. If products and services add more value for customers than you thought they would, consider increasing prices. Of course, there are a number of obstacles to consider. There are several reasons for this.

Move from a Revenue to a Profit Focus

One of the most destructive myths of business is that if you grow the top line by increasing sales, you will see increased profits. The myth, simply stated, is "If you worry about the sales, profits will take care of themselves." The myth encourages managers to lower prices for the sake of increasing sales. The problem is that this myth, like most myths, will eventually lead to consequences precisely the opposite of what they promise. What makes this a business myth is the unstated assumption behind it. The assumption is that product or service delivery teams will effectively keep costs down. This perception causes managers to initiate pricing decisions to increase revenue that may eventually lead to the decline of profits and, in some markets, actually decrease sales when those markets are mature.

Salespeople often honor this myth to close orders. After all, salespeople are trained to close sales. They're supposed to be hungry. It's natural for them to lower price to close a sale. Even if it means giving up all of the profit, they are willing to make a sale with a lower price. From the salespersons' perspective, they're doing what they have been trained to do. Salespeople are usually compensated and managed to sacrifice profits for revenue. Senior managers add to the problem with their focus on monthly or quarterly revenue numbers and their willingness to sacrifice profits through lower prices to achieve revenue goals.

The myth exposes pricing in the trenches, the moment when a deal seems to be in jeopardy because of price. In the trenches, it's difficult to have confidence in your prices, to confidently walk away from a sale. It's so difficult that many managers make decisions that may or may not increase sales and definitely undermine profits. Let's look at a hypothetical example of how this happens.

A manager we'll call Paul Warren is the general manager of Orion Electronics, a company which produces a digital voltage regulator used in aircraft engines. Orion sells 1,000 units at a selling price of $100 each. Orion's sales manager has requested authority to offer a price discount of $10 per unit and has projected that they will be able to increase sales by 15 percent. Looking at Figure 5.1, if Orion lowers the unit price to $90, and sales increase to 1,150 units, revenue increases from $100,000 to $103,500, or 3.5 percent. Most sales managers would agree that a 3.5 percent increase in revenues is significant.

Now, let's look at the profit implications of increasing revenue. Due to the variable cost of $40 per unit (labor, parts, testing, packaging, and shipping), Orion saw that increased volume raised variable costs from $40,000 to $46,000, an increase of 15 percent. Machine and plant costs remain fixed despite the increased volume. So when Paul Warren looked at the bottom line resulting from the decision, profits actually declined by $6,000.

We know that profit analysis is rarely as simple as this. Your costing systems are much more complex and show much more detail. But the point we want to make applies equally to both simple and complex analyses: managers often sacrifice profits for the sake of revenue. They factor in all kinds of justifications as to why lower

Price	$100	$90
Forecasted Units	1,000	1,150
Forecasted Revenue	$100,000	$103,500
Costs:		
Variable	$40,000	$46,000
Plant & Equip.	$50,000	$50,000
Total	$90,000	$96,000
Net Profit	$10,000	$4,000

Figure 5.1   Orion Electronics 10% Price Discount Analysis.

profits are desirable or even unavoidable. We've heard all the excuses. Customers are smarter. Competitors are more aggressive. Products are becoming commoditized. The list of reasons is longer than this book. Some of them are even valid. Sure, it is harder to negotiate. Customers have better information. All true. But the reality is that managers need to focus on the profits of a product line as well as on the sales revenue.

Let's go back to Orion Electronics. Knowing what you know now, what's your advice for Paul Warren? Should he agree to give up $6,000 in profits for the sake of $3,500 in revenue? Of course not. Yet, managers make these kinds of decisions all the time and will routinely sacrifice profits for revenue. How do we change that? One solution is to change compensation systems. At some level, managers need to be evaluated on their ability to increase profits. One way is by developing metrics and analytics around contribution dollars that go toward the fixed expenses of the company.

Efficiency First

In order for you to have confidence in your prices, they must be backed up by an efficient infrastructure of processes and products. If it takes a competitor one hour to perform an activity you do in two hours, pricing is the least of your concerns. Efficiencies must be competitive for costs to be competitive. And, if the quality of the work performed by your workers is significantly better, then the situation changes for salespeople. Now they can sell quality, not just price. But the main point remains: If your company isn't cost competitive, it's in trouble and that's got to be fixed.

This is the situation Caterpillar faced when Komatsu entered the U.S. construction equipment market. With a union labor force and very high production costs, Caterpillar could not easily reduce costs. To solve the problem, it became more efficient. Caterpillar appealed to the union to relax restrictive work rules. Together, the company and the union found better ways to squeeze production out of the same number of workers. The company boosted automation and improved product quality. In one of the most celebrated examples of corporate turnaround, Caterpillar improved its efficiency, reduced its costs, and became competitive in the global marketplace. As a result, they once again dominate the heavy construction equipment market.

Private equity firms are pretty smart. Lots of people wonder why they would buy a struggling auto parts operation. These are companies that have supplied some of the best price buyers in the world to Detroit's once Big Three car manufacturers. To make matters worse, the auto parts company faces fierce competition, tough unions, and out-of-date plants. On the surface, it certainly seems like a bad bet.

The reason the private equity firms want to buy this kind of company is quite simple. They know that with better and tougher management, they can turn it into a cash machine. The private equity firms learned the lessons that Caterpillar and the computer assembly companies learned in the 1980s: A revitalized management team focused on efficient operations and leveraging value for clients will win the day. Is it tough to do that? Sure. Being tough is what business is all about these days. Unions are tough, customers are tough, and managers need to be tough. Especially when it comes to running an efficient business. Investors know that replacing managers who have become victims of circumstances with those who choose to control issues is a winning and profitable idea.

The Cost of Average Costing

Another problem that gets in the way of profitable pricing is your costing system. It tends to average costs over multiple products and allocates fixed costs to products in a way that can actually cause your most profitable products to be vulnerable to competition. When the competitors attack, they will almost always use price, and when you look at your costing sheets, you think the competitor is selling below their cost. But, in fact, the competitor is just smarter at using price to leverage their assets. It often comes in very simple areas such as how you analyze a potential new piece of business. Let's look at an example.

Wilson Enterprises provides contract consultants for logistics services in the travel industry. Its consultants generally invoice $200 per hour. Current volume is 100,000 hours per year. Wilson consultants earn $120 per hour. Expenses for marketing and computer support are $5 million and $1 million per year for administration. A new customer, Hawaiian Adventures, has asked Wilson to provide contract services on a long-term basis but wants to pay $160 per hour rather than $200. In return, Hawaiian Adventures will guarantee Wilson Enterprises 25,000 hours per year. It will also agree to accept support from Wilson's Idaho support center where Wilson consultants are paid $110 per hour. Wilson Enterprises' incremental costs to service this account will be $500,000 (for additional computer capacity) and $125,000 (for administrative overhead).

The manager at Wilson must decide if the Hawaiian Adventures program will be profitable. Before we give our recommendation, follow our analysis. Most companies put all of their fixed costs into a pool and average those costs across all products. When averaging these costs, they may seem to be variable with changes in volume when they really are not. Further, the averaged costs make it look like some business opportunities don't add incremental profits when in fact they do. Let's look at the costs as part of this decision in a few different ways. In Figure 5.2, we see this potential sales order the way many companies allocate their fixed costs—by averaging them. We've added computer and administrative costs, then added them into the fixed cost pool and averaged them across all products.

The result in Figure 5.2 is that the new opportunity has a fixed cost allocation of $44 for computer costs and $9 for administrative and overhead. The total cost of $163 means that the business opportunity appears to be losing $3 per hour of volume. A smart manager would not take the business.

Now, let's take a look at what would happen to Wilson Enterprises' *total* profit if it did take the order from Hawaiian Adventures,

	Hawaiian Adv. Opportunity
Revenue	$160
Costs:	
Variable	($110)
Computer	($44)
Administrative	($9)
Total	($163)
Net Loss	($3)

Figure 5.2   Wilson Enterprises Full Cost Approach.

even if it meant losing $3 per hour. Figure 5.3 shows the aggregate effect of actually accepting the business.

The analysis in Figure 5.3 shows an incremental $625,000 in net profits. These profits were hidden in the averaging of costs across all products. It's important to be able to isolate the profit components across a portfolio of products and services. This can be difficult information to get when making pricing decisions that will allow a company to take deals that will increase the profits of the business.

	Current	Added	New Total
Revenue	$20,000,000	$4,000,000	$24,000,000
Costs:			
Variable	($12,000,000)	($2,750,000)	($14,750,000)
Computer	($5,000,000)	($500,000)	($5,500,000)
Administrative	($1,000,000)	($125,000)	($1,125,000)
Total	($18,000,000)		($21,375,000)
Net Profit (Loss)	$2,000,000		$2,625,000

Figure 5.3   Wilson Enterprises Total Company Analysis.

The solution is to deal only with costs that are incremental in the analysis. By incremental costs, we mean only those that result from taking the additional order. In the case of Wilson Enterprises, the resulting incremental analysis is shown in Figure 5.4.

The incremental cost analysis shows the real impact of the Hawaiian Enterprises sales order in added revenue *and* profits. Because Wilson Enterprises did not have to allocate fixed or existing cost information, getting the answer was actually easier than prior analyses. That's the great thing about incremental costing. It is easier to identify and understand the information for all parties involved in the deal.

Think about this analysis from a competitive perspective. Let's say there were two competitors, each looking at the Hawaiian Adventures opportunity. If Company A looked at the information with average costs, they would turn the sales order down because it looked unprofitable. Company B takes the business, and their average costs get lower. Company A's average costs would eventually be higher, and as a result they would suspect their prices would have to go up. They may even think that their competitor was nuts to take the business. In reality, their own average costs are nuts.

	Added Costs & Revenue	Per-Hour Results of New Opportunity
Revenue	$4,000,000	$160
Costs:		
Variable	($2,750,000)	($110)
Computer	($500,000)	($20)
Administrative	($125,000)	($5)
Total	($3,375,000)	($135)
Profit (Loss)	$625,000	$25

Figure 5.4   Wilson Enterprises Incremental Cost Analysis Approach.

Company B considered the sales order incrementally, and thus might be inclined to take it and get the benefit of the increased revenue and profitability. Plus they would get the added benefit of having a footprint in the lower-value marketplace. That way, they keep their lower-value competitors fighting for business at the low end rather than letting them get comfortably established in this spot and eventually move into the high-end market.

When managers average costs, it puts them at a competitive disadvantage when making pricing moves against those competitors that don't. This is because their business opportunities look less profitable than they really are. The companies that look at incremental costs will always have a true picture of the profit coming from any piece of potential business.

We once saw the problem of averaging costs play out in a decentralized corporation with a number of large divisions. At Division A, the decision was to calculate incremental costs; at Division B, the decision was to fully allocate costs. Over time, this company began shifting most production to Division A, the incrementally costed facility. The problem was that Division B had extensive fixed investments in plant and equipment. Once Division A began producing products costed incrementally, it actually caused more and more sales orders to move to their division and led to the demise of Division B. Thinking Division B could never be profitable, corporate management eventually sold the division to another company for a discount, and the facility was closed. What a waste.

An example of a company that does incremental costing quite well is Exxon Mobil. It continually adjusts capacity to take advantage of demand. And, it adjusts price to better leverage capacity. Sure, that adjustment takes time and is costly. But that effort brings many times its cost in added revenue and profits. Exxon Mobil is great at fine-tuning prices to fully utilize the dynamic capacity it can place online. And that capacity is increased when necessary to keep up with increases in demand and shutdown during market downturns.

Incremental costs are especially important for professional services companies such as consulting firms, accounting firms, and law firms. The capacity costs of people and/or of fixed facilities for hotels and airlines, for example, tend to be a larger portion of their cost structure than corresponding costs for manufacturing companies. Those costs tend to be fixed over the short term, especially if people are not going to be separated when utilization is low. Furthermore, unused human capacity is very volatile. Just like the value of an unfilled airline seat goes to zero the instant the airplane door shuts, the value of a lost day of untapped human capacity to drive revenue and profits evaporates forever.

Costing systems will either help you or hurt you if your pricing purpose is to increase profits. They do that by either preventing or allowing you to accept business that increases the overall profits of the company. Many managers are aware of this approach and its importance, but avoid it because they worry that salespeople may start discounting deals down to the level of the incremental costs and all of their business will migrate there. Their concerns are justified. Fortunately, there is a solution for this concern. The insight to the solution comes from looking at how the airlines price. Considering the current financial state of many airlines, you might think they are lousy pricers, and some are. But if you understand and apply the premise of how they price seats and a few of their lessons, you'll do just fine.

Price Like the Airlines—Almost

On January 17, 1985, American Airlines rolled out the first revenue management pricing system. This was the airlines' answer to the fierce price competition that resulted from deregulation. The deregulation of the airline industry gave a number of lower-cost competitors the chance to enter the business and pick and choose the most profitable routes in which to compete. The legacy airlines (e.g., American, United, and Delta), those around during the early years when costs could be passed on to consumers, were suddenly at a significant disadvantage since they had signed expensive contracts with the unions of their pilots, cabin attendants, and mechanics. They desperately needed a better way to compete with the low-cost upstarts. Revenue management was the solution.

Revenue management is the process of increasing the flow of revenue or contribution dollars through scarce resources such as an aircraft. Contribution dollars represent the revenue that flows from the sale of products and services after incremental costs are paid. Contribution dollars must then pay for the cost of fixed expenses like plant and equipment. It is useful to think of contribution or margin dollars as a flow that has to fill up buckets that represent costs. The first bucket is the variable cost, the second bucket is the fixed expenses, and the final bucket is profits. The flow of revenue dollars fills the variable cost bucket, the overflow is the contribution dollars that flow into the fixed cost bucket and, if we do our jobs right, fill up the profit bucket to a reasonable level. If we make pricing decisions with an understanding of what it will take to increase the flow of contribution dollars of an individual product, or for the business in aggregate, we will improve the net profits and margins of the business. That's how you move to a profit focus in a business. That's what revenue management seeks to do.

Revenue management has been massaged by quant jocks that fine-tuned the initial lessons of Delta and American into sophisticated software tools used to extract every possible penny per sale of a seat. For the rest of us, there are some basic lessons about how the airlines and hotels run their pricing that are important for marketing, pricing, and sales managers to understand. They are good lessons on how to run a business that has relatively fixed capacity and variable demand such as manufacturing, professional services, transportation, lodging, and hospitality. These lessons fit into a great conceptual structure for how we should think of using price to increase both capacity utilization and profits. The net result is to increase company returns.

Let's say that airlines have, in effect, three classes of products: first class, business class, and tourist fares. In fact, they actually have dozens for each flight. With at least two weeks' notice, a first class seat from Boston to San Francisco is approximately $1,600. A passenger can buy a refundable ticket in the economy section for about $800. And if the passenger is willing to take the risk of buying a restricted (nonrefundable) fare, the cost might be $300 or even less.

Businesspeople are willing to pay $800 for an unrestricted economy class seat when the same seat can be obtained for $300. That's because the average businessperson is less price sensitive than the casual flier. But there is another reason. The airlines exploit pricing by erecting barriers or fences to the lower-cost seats that makes them less preferable to travelers who pay the higher fares. Businesspeople are willing to pay more to make last-minute changes, to not have to stay over on a Saturday night, and to get priority rebooking if their flight is canceled.

There are plenty of businesspeople to fill up the $800 seats on Monday and Friday. Airlines sell the cheap seats when they wouldn't otherwise sell them at a higher price—during the times when fewer businesspeople travel, such as on Wednesday. The airline's objective is to make sure they maximize the contribution dollars on each flight. During peak times, they can fill the aircraft with businesspeople coming home from a week of travel for $800 per seat. In the off period, when there are fewer businesspeople traveling, they would rather sell a limited number of seats for $250 than have the seat unoccupied when the airplane door shuts. Of course they *fence* the price with programs like Saturday night stay-overs to ensure that businesspeople are less likely to buy the cheaper seats on the same flight.

When airlines see they are going to have excess capacity on a flight, their yield management system adjusts prices dynamically— hundreds or thousands of times per day—to maximize revenue per flight. Rather than offer discounts to customers who would book a seat at the higher fare, the airlines offer excess capacity to travelers who would otherwise not have flown. They try to do this without undermining the structure of the high-value users of the service.

To further increase revenue, the airlines keep a number of first class seats available for last-minute travelers. The airline knows it can command a premium for these seats. This is because last-minute business travelers tend to be significantly less price sensitive than leisure travelers. There's always a risk to the airlines, of course, that these last-minute seats will not, in fact, find buyers. In this case, the airlines up-sell or give the seats away to reward their most loyal frequent fliers.

You would think that with all of this going on, the airlines would be quite profitable. In the early years of using prices to increase revenues, the airlines made billions of dollars of extra profits. Over time, those profits disappeared and only the low-cost airlines like Southwest and Jet Blue are consistently making money. That's because of a little flaw in revenue management. It measures short-term willingness to pay. When it does that, it thinks that loyal travelers are less price sensitive. It charges those loyal travelers more and more as it charges leisure travelers less and less. Over time, the difference can grow to be over 300 percent. We call that dumbbell pricing.

Dumbbell Pricing

It's called *dumbbell pricing* because you end up with two extremes of customers, both getting the same basic service but each paying dramatically different prices. The unsuspecting customers at the top eventually realize that they are being taken advantage of and begin to try the lower-cost airlines. They discover that the lower-cost airlines may have nicer, roomier seats with real leather. The food is better and the amenities are attractive, even live TV and satellite radio at each seat. Eventually, these loyal customers switch to another airline and when they do, the original airline has to sell more discount seats and may lose money on the flight. The take-away? In order to make money using yield management, it takes a stable or growing group of high-value and/or loyal customers who pay a higher price.

Any airline or any other business that takes unfair advantage of its loyal customers is going to lose their loyal base. The no-frills airlines like Southwest and Jet Blue have differential fares of only

$50 to $75 from high price to low price, and those fares are published right on their web sites so everyone knows that they're being treated fairly.

To avoid the loss of loyal customers, the airlines need to rationalize their prices at the high and low levels. And, they need to get their cost structure and operational efficiencies in line with the realities of today's business environment. This is what American Airlines has been doing with a lot of success over the past several years. Without following suit, we suggest that the others will continue to lose business to the low-cost airlines and at increasing rates. Making these changes is easier said than done, but it is the only way they'll survive.

Using Price to Control Utilization

Some important lessons can be learned from the airlines in using price to improve profits. Sure, the airlines are dealing with individual consumers, and you're dealing with big corporations that have experienced buyers who know how to exert control. But chances are if you find the right fence, or way to insulate the value of your high-end offerings, that even marquee companies will value, you will be surprised at how fast you can use prices to increase both utilization and profits. The trick is to use price to fill capacity but to do it in a way that keeps the high-value customers paying fair but high prices, and prevents them from wanting to take advantage of the low-value offering. And you want to make sure you don't let a low-value customer bump a high-value one.

A number of years ago, we were working with a technology company that had a wide range of products, some of them custom high-value products, others rock bottom commodities. These were the products they were losing money on and that were being sold by 20 other competitors. The marketing manager for the product told us how one of their major customers had sent the company jet to pick up their monthly allocation of the product. Wow, something was going on in this business, and a commodity was suddenly a high-value product. We suggested that they raise their prices, but they said they couldn't because most of the purchases were under contract. Fortunately, the delivery time wasn't under contract.

The company introduced a new product that was available from stock at a 60 percent premium over the ones that were taking 16 weeks to deliver. The customer's response was "We wondered when you were going to figure out what was going on in this business." No complaints, just gratitude for having parts available. The real punch line was that these customers were the automobile companies—companies that use aggressive price negotiations.

To make it work, managers need to adopt three very different pricing approaches as shown in Figure 5.5. They are used based on the utilization of the resources of the company, be they machines or people. It is useful to think of each approach as being in a zone of utilization.

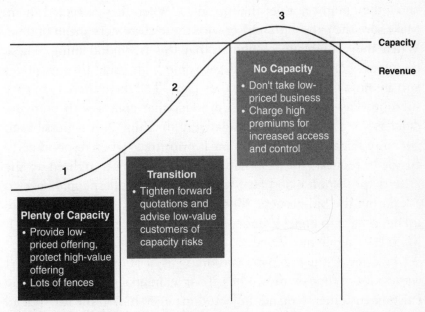

Figure 5.5 Using Price to Control Utilization.

Zone 1 in Figure 5.5 represents the period when there is ample capacity. What many companies do during these periods is reduce the price of their high-value products. By doing so, they undermine the value structure of the company and their credibility with customers when the business cycle improves. Instead, the company should introduce low-value products or reduce service levels from the high-value package. Good examples would be to add clauses into marginal customer contracts that include unpredictable lead times, limited or fee-based technical support, and bulk packaging. The point is that there has to be something that fences or insulates the low-value customers from high-value customers. Guaranteed delivery is often a good fence for both products and services. This is critical to put in place prior to the upswing. The job of the fence is to protect the high-value offering. The job of the low-value offering is to improve the utilization of business resources, which should go away when those resources are fully used.

Zone 2 is the transition period. When there are signs that the business is beginning to come back, let the low-value customers know they might not get their products when they expected them. Make sure the expectation is set with these customers ahead of time. When they complain, recognize that this is a good thing. These customers believed they could get some high value for low prices and are now disappointed that they can't. Tell them there is an easy solution. Pay for the premium product that comes with premium delivery, or pay for expedited delivery. In Zone 2, it is possible to get more selective about how time is prioritized when responding to customer requests for proposals. This is the time to tighten up the criteria for response and qualify questions that salespeople need to ask during the bid process. Most customers don't think that they're going to have to knuckle under at this point and end up regretting it when they move into Zone 3.

In Zone 3, the company is running at or above capacity. Don't waste a lot of time on most RFPs. Your main goal should be meeting existing customer demand. In fact, don't even bid on the low-priced opportunities because now there is a need to reserve capacity to satisfy high-value customers. Remember how the airlines reserve some first-class seats for last-minute travelers? Always have a little extra capacity to take on the real high-value business, whether it be through an extra shift or weekend work. Costs will be a little higher, but the company should be charging a premium for customers to get capacity access during these times.

The fractional jet ownership business has been one of the great success stories in aviation over the last decade. Started by NetJets, the program enables individuals or corporations to *own* fractions—as little as one-sixteenth—of a light jet. There are many advantages to sharing the costs of an airplane. Most owners do not expect to use an airplane for the 400 hours per year needed to justify its full ownership. They are willing to pay on a per-hour basis for the convenience of having access to a jet. The fractional jet companies are able to optimize the use of these jets in a way that individual owners cannot. It's no coincidence that investment guru Warren Buffett purchased NetJets.

But, though demand for fractional jet ownership is growing, managers are finding profits elusive. This is because the growth has caused unbalanced demand for the jets. If a client asks for access to a jet when other clients are in physical possession of it, the supplier is contract-bound to satisfy the client's requirements even if it means leasing a jet from another charter operation. If the cost to lease the jet exceeds the fees the client has paid, the supplier has to absorb the loss.

Given this reality, how should fractional jet companies price their services? A number of options present themselves. One pricing strategy to balance the load factor is to lower prices to encourage users who can shift their demand away from peak periods. Or they could impose a price premium to get access to a jet during peak periods. Either approach would cause a smoothing of demand and higher profits for the leasing companies.

To make matters worse, several of the leasing companies purchased too many jets, and they're using low prices to fill capacity. They figure that if the big airlines can use price to fill seats, so can they. Here's the rub. The big airlines use low price to fill seats, not airplanes. The leasing companies are using low price to fill the whole plane. The difference for a big airplane is that the incremental cost of filling a seat is peanuts. The incremental cost of putting a jet in the air, even a small one, is high fuel, a crew, and associated costs for engine and equipment wear and tear. Using low price when the incremental cost is high is dangerous, since it is not likely to provide positive profit contribution.

Any time a company is anticipating growth, they're going to enter a period of turbulence. To survive the turbulence, they've got to prepare for it before they hit it. They need to make sure they have a good understanding of how price can be used to shift capacity before they need to do it. The point is that they've got to do both or they won't be flying too long.

Companies that should use this approach are any industry that has cycles of use leading to capacity constraints and cost structures that are or can be high contribution. Some industries, such as steel and pulp and paper industries do this in a reactive manner by reducing prices on high-value products and services. They leave significant amounts of money on the table by not being proactive about managing the capacity process and introducing low-value services and products with long lead times.

One industry that should use opportunity costing to control utilization is the professional services business. Managers in the professional services industry tend to look at their labor as a high variable cost when, in many cases, their costs are really fixed. To the extent that they are willing to separate employees if there is a downturn, the employees represent a variable cost. However, the core group of people who are protected from separation are a fixed cost and should therefore be viewed that way in both the costing and the pricing process.

For those companies, traditional costing approaches can lead to a number of severe strategic problems. First, they tend to drop prices on high-value services and lose money on them. The trick is to offer lower prices but to make sure some level of service and support is taken out of the offering. The second problem is that they permit customers to focus on costs in a world where increased globalization has caused plenty of high-value professional resources to be available from traditionally low-cost cultures like India and China. Companies that use those resources are able to compete effectively on a cost basis with companies that do not.

For companies that don't have access to those resources and perhaps even some that do, cost-based competition misses the point. Most professional resources provide value to clients. By focusing on the value that professional resources bring to clients and learning to improve that value, professional services companies are able to move out of the cost-based meat grinder of customer negotiations and into the value-based discussion with higher-level client executives that provides more benefit to everyone involved.

ADD NEW PRODUCTS AND SERVICES THAT GIVE YOU NEGOTIATING FLEXIBILITY AND GROWTH

Provide your salespeople with the gives and gets that are so important in negotiating. If customers want a lower price, subtract features and services. Capture the value of valuable services. When products are regarded as commodities, add services to differentiate products and prop up prices. This strategy is undermined when valuable services are given away. To gain more confidence in negotiating, you can price incremental services to reflect their true value to customers. An effective strategy for market dominance is to develop a dual offering that covers both the high- and low-end customer needs. Flanking offerings grow both the revenue and the global footprint of the firm.

P ricing is important to businesses, but it's not the most important thing. Businesses need to grow. Like sharks, which must move forward in order to stay alive, businesses need to add innovative products and services, identify new markets, and create new opportunities for revenue and profit. A disciplined pricing strategy is an important means to that end. But the emphasis must be on innovation to boost revenues and profits. Pricing with confidence will help capture the value that your business creates, but without something to capture, even the most brilliant pricing strategy can't help you.

Companies that lack the ability to innovate face serious problems. Without new products and services in the pipeline, businesses are reduced to having but one lever to drive growth—pricing. These businesses push for higher prices in the hope that their customers will accept the price increases. The fear, of course, is that customers will bolt in the face of direct price increases. Some businesses try to finesse the issue by implementing back-door price increases in the form of layered fees and service charges. This has happened in banking and financial services and is currently happening in the shipping business. We know that banking institutions are not entirely comfortable with this approach because customers who complain about specific fees can usually negotiate them away. Why? Because the businesses know that without innovative offerings, they have little leverage. They can't afford to lose existing customers, so they agree to subtract the fees.

Continually driving price and fee increases and then negotiating to give most of them back just makes things worse. The practice sends mixed messages and undermines already weak value positioning and puts even more pressure on sales teams to negotiate price. And, it makes customers who used to be loyal become either price buyers or poker players. It's a vicious cycle that is shared by many organizations. In this rule, we'll show you how to break that cycle.

The Problem with Using Pricing to Drive Growth

An overreliance on pricing to drive growth damages relationships with your customers. The banking crisis of the early 1980s made financial institutions desperate to improve profits. The focus of those efforts, often recommended by outside consultants, was to improve underwriting standards. But improving underwriting standards is hard work. Wasn't there anything a little bit easier? Indeed there was, the consultants agreed. The banks could simply add fees, service charges, and penalties. The net result was predictable. The banks made some short-term profits, but they also alienated loyal customers and forced all customers to become totally price-oriented. Customers were trained to switch their banking relationships for the best deal of the week. In the end, the commoditization of the banking business was complete.

We see the same dynamic in the air cargo business, a brutally competitive sector driven by price. The air cargo carriers have also learned that they can be competitive on published rates but only if they tack on an array of fees for fuel, inspections, and a host of other things. For the time being, air cargo companies enjoy a critical mass of loyal customers who regard the air cargo companies as logistics partners. High switching costs currently make it impractical for many customers to abandon their existing air cargo partners. But as billing becomes more transparent and customers absorb the impact of these fees, many customers *will* bolt.

Luckily, there's a practical solution to avoid the vicious cycle. Businesses must be able to present a dual-level bundling approach that has a low-price, bare-bones offering and a higher-price, full-service offering. This solution prevents alienation of loyal customers and also gives salespeople some choices when selling to poker players to better ferret out their position. In most markets, as we saw in Rule Four, there are more value- or relationship-oriented customers than price-oriented customers. It often doesn't seem like that, because suppliers do so many things like tacking on surcharges that cause customers not to trust us. When that happens, all customers act like price buyers. And why not? The businesses trained the customers how to do it.

Innovate for Growth, Price for Profits

To break the cycle you need to *innovate for growth* and *price for profits*. Here's what we mean. If you want to improve your pricing leverage, some element of your offerings must be differentiated. If your offerings aren't differentiated, they are commodities and the lowest price gets the business. The challenge for many firms is that their core offerings *are* commodities—or close to it. That's fine. There are customers that have basic needs. For the rest of your markets, you need something more to differentiate yourself from the competition. In addition to high-value products, much of this differentiation will come from services.

The global steel industry is a great setting to see how this plays out. Steel, a technology developed around 1000 BC, is as pure a commodity as one can find. Large global competitors are buying up smaller basic steel plants around the world with the aim of dominating price-based competition. Yet niche opportunities for premium prices abound. Argentina's Tenaris SA provides high-value seamless steel pipes used in offshore drilling operations around the world—an application enjoying soaring demand as the petroleum industry moves deeper and deeper offshore.

The growth of this market makes it attractive for the global giants, who can offer very low prices to customers. In contrast Tenaris bundles high-value-added services with its premium steel pipes—a strategy that has been effective at keeping these global giants out of the market. Tenaris bundles advanced technical support, engineering, just-in-time deliveries that help its customers improve their exploration and production operations. Their understanding of the way their customers operate—economically, technologically, and environmentally—differentiates them from the price-oriented steel conglomerates.

The net result? Tenaris and the niche players are able to command and protect prices of $2,000 per ton, over three times the prices the global commodity players battle over. Their understanding of customer operations and priorities enables them to gain far higher profitability margins and keep the titans at bay.

The Basics of a Good Offering Structure

To create high-impact offerings, set out some basic objectives. These should include:

- Matching offerings with the high-value needs of target customer segments.
- Offering low-value flanking products that appeal to price-sensitive customers and reduce the effects of price negotiations on high-value offerings.
- Meeting or beating competitive performance on core customer needs.
- Building strong fences between high- and low-value offerings that prevent customers from negotiating for high-value offerings at low prices.
- Enabling sales to have clear discussions with customers to define price-value trade-offs during negotiations.
- Arming sales with well-defined value levers to alter offering value and price by adding or removing specific features.

Consider the case of Intuit and its QuickBooks financial management software. Intuit offers five different versions of the software that vary according to standard and optional features and delivery mechanism (hosted versus customer installed). The key elements of each offering, summarized in Figure 6.1, define straightforward price-value combinations for customers.

An essential benefit of well-defined offering levels is that it enables your sales teams to better control price negotiations. Having both high- and low-value offerings puts sales in the driver's seat during price negotiations. If they are pressured to lower the price, they can offer the customer the low-value product. For some, the low-value offering will better meet their needs and budget so they'll buy it. On the other hand, most poker-playing customers will react

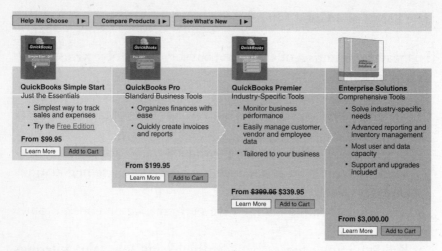

Figure 6.1   The Intuit QuickBooks Product Portfolio.

with indignation. They do this because the salesperson has called their bluff and exposed their true intention: getting the high-value offering for a low price.

The reality of managing the poker game is that it is a little bit more complicated than just having one high-value and one low-value offering. After all, you have multiple segments to serve. And each customer within those segments may have unique needs. Setting up sales to control the poker game and better manage pricing requires creating more options for price-value trade-offs. To do this, it is helpful to think of constructing offerings with three levels: core offerings, expected offerings, and value-added options. Let's consider each in turn.

Core Offerings

Core offerings are the minimum set of attributes to make the offering viable across the majority of all customers. Anderson and Narus refer to this as a "naked solution" and define it as "the bare minimum of products and services that all segment members uniformly value."[1] For most companies it is also helpful to relate this core offering to the concept of a common technology platform. A good example is the publicly available, unsupported version of Linux. For companies that have the internal resources to use the software, it is free. If they want help and specialized applications, they have to purchase them from a variety of vendors like Red Hat.

The core offering enables companies to generate incremental margin dollars by serving the low end of the market. Sticking to a true core offering to do this also protects against price erosion from higher-value customers who cannot trade down because they need the associated features, capabilities, and services. It is also a critical tool in controlling upstart competitors that often enter markets with low-cost and low-value products.

Expected Offerings

Expected offerings add things to the core to meet the needs of specific segments. Its objective is to appeal to the majority of customers within that segment. The expected offering is comprised of features and service levels desired by the majority of customers in a given segment. It is what customers typically ask for and what is required of most suppliers in order to be considered credible. It includes extra features or services that often include "terms, delivery, support efforts and (access to) new ideas."[2]

Value-Added Options

Even though the logic of high- to low-value product offerings is compelling, it is not enough. Most firms are facing commoditization of their core products. Finding it harder to stay ahead of the competition, the smart ones have invested heavily in creating *value-added options:* services, consulting operations, and capabilities for outsourcing entire business processes. Those that succeed create a cadre of loyal customers, high competitive barriers, and confidence in their prices because they are creating superior value for their customers. Some of the service innovators have actually been at it a very long time. Traditional product companies like GE and Air Products began developing their successful models many years ago.

The Critical Role of Services and Solutions

As we saw, Intuit uses services to augment their tiered product offerings. Let's take a closer look at how Intuit structures services as part of its pricing strategy (see Figure 6.2).

The addition of services gives Intuit an additional means to manage price negotiations. In addition to high- to low-value software offerings, Intuit sales teams can add or remove services to simultaneously meet customer needs and better manage pricing.

Results show there is a pot of gold out there for those firms that can execute a multilevel offering strategy that includes products, services, and software or data and analytics. Under Lou Gerstner,

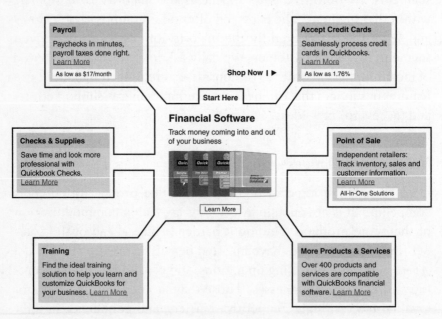

Figure 6.2   Services Provide Greater Price-Value Trade-Offs.

IBM set out on this course and transformed itself from a hardware-centric organization to one that emphasized services and solutions, of which hardware is a part. IBM recognized the commoditization of its mainframe computers and increased its focus on the software and services it wraps around those systems. After building up their own software business, they began buying smaller companies, integrating them well, and accelerating their growth by taking advantage of IBM's mammoth sales force.

Companies that undervalue software and services often find themselves in a cycle of desperation. Because of commoditization of their core offerings, pricing pressure increases. To try to stem price erosion, services are added but are often given away. As Figure 6.3 shows, costs go up while revenue continues to decline.

We see many firms going through this cycle. Managers get frustrated because along the way, customers begin to expect to get free services to accommodate for the commoditized product. This is especially true when competitors begin to catch up, first with the product improvements and then with the added services. Clearly, you need to get paid for the high-value services that you provide when you start providing them. The challenge is that some basic level of service is usually required. Let's look at how to sort this all out.

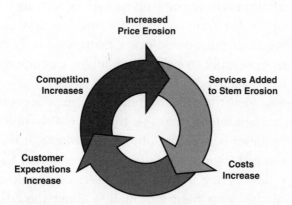

Figure 6.3   The Services Commoditization Cycle.

Developing Services and Solutions to Create Pricing Leverage

An easy way to start is to put your services into one of two categories. The first category is *enabling services* such as maintenance and support, postdelivery training, or predelivery design support. These types of services are often expected to be available and that expectation is often misinterpreted as an unwillingness to pay for them. The rationalization to give them away is almost always the same: "We have to include those services to ensure that the product performs." But customers will pay for them, and, accordingly, they should be an explicit part of the offering and price menus.

If you hear the tired old story about "We *have* to include those services," ask yourself two basic questions. First, "At what level should our services perform?" Second, "What is the financial impact for customers of different levels of performance?" The answers to these questions do two things. They force a definition of the boundaries between the expected and value-added levels for services, and they enable identification of your customers who are seeking high and low value.

The second category of services are *high-value adds* and are often components of solutions to specific customer business problems. Companies such as Deluxe and John Harland that sell checks to banks and consumers have come up with an interesting way to drive new revenues as their core check printing business continues to decline. They offer outsourced order management. Each provides a special call-in number to help new banking customers select and order their checks and accompanying accessories.

Most banks view the process of opening a new account as one of the most important interactions that they have with their customers. Since the customer is typically physically present in the bank and is highly engaged, banks want their representatives to make the most of the time. They train customer service people extensively on how to gather important information about the customer and make initial pitches to cross-sell other products, such as home equity lines and auto loans. Up-selling customers to more expensive check designs is a source of profits. But since selling checks would take away from the time available to sell more profitable products, banks are happy to outsource this step to specialists at the check printer. There is often considerable pricing pressure on the core product (the box of checks), so such services represent significant profit growth opportunities for the check providers.

Combining these two different types of services with products and financing services can lead to the creation of powerful solutions for customers. Consider General Electric and its design of the GE90 aircraft engine. Introduced in the late 1980s for the then-promising market for twin-engine, long-haul passenger jets such as the Boeing 777, the GE90 was a completely new design competing against older offerings from Pratt & Whitney and Rolls-Royce. Using new, exotic materials and engineering advances, the GE90 was a technological marvel. In its early days, it was also a commercial failure.

What happened? It turns out that GE hadn't done its homework in the area of customer value. While its engines were technically superior, GE, to its surprise, lost deal after deal to Pratt & Whitney and Rolls-Royce. GE finally got around to asking the right questions. What it found was that customers were reluctant to take the risk of change. They chose a product they knew over a product they didn't because with experience came predictable total costs of ownership. The GE90 had no track record, and its application of advanced technology and materials, the very attributes GE managers saw as benefits, were what many customers regarded as financial risks.

How did GE respond? First GE created an entire solution around the GE90 that simultaneously addressed customers' financial concerns (their value needs) and thereby demonstrated significant competitive advantage. The new solution called "Power by the Hour" tapped into the old practice of leasing capital equipment so that customers could pay for a fully maintained and operational engine. Furthermore, they could elect to pay GE by aircraft operating hour. In this way, GE aligned the way customers pay for value with how they accumulate value. (Customers, of course, could do business the traditional way by buying engines.)

In the early 1990s, GE had approximately 25 percent share in the market for commercial aircraft engines. By the late 1990s, GE Engine Leasing had won half of all the orders for new engines. By 2004, GE emerged as the market leader in worldwide commercial engine sales, with a 40 percent market share, followed by Pratt & Whitney and Rolls-Royce at 30 percent each. And, GE is the exclusive supplier of engines for the Boeing 777.

Why Good Fences Make Good Neighbors

When we talk with product managers about the importance of low-value flanking products and value-adding services, they express two very real concerns. The first is fear that if they introduce a low-value offering that it will cannibalize demand for their higher-value offerings. The second is that they will not be able to control access to services. If either of these happens, it could wreak havoc with their P&L. The key to addressing both of these problems is to create a series of *fences* that prevent this from happening.

One of the main reasons for having a logical, disciplined offering structure is to prevent customers from obtaining high-value offerings for unjustified low prices. The basic elements of the offering structure must enable the creation of fences to make this happen. A *fence* is just what it sounds like: a means to protect the price integrity of offerings by forcing a trade-off between price and value.

Creating good fences is another one of those overlooked areas where good managers can build value for their organizations. The key is to pick criteria that will withstand all-out assaults by poker-playing customers and will be supported by senior management. Common examples of strong fences include distinct differences in product features, sales channels, service and support, logistics, and brand. Providers of information products use timeliness of access, depth of information, ability to perform analysis, catalog data, and format. The good news is that the rules for creating actionable fences are very simple.

1. Fences must be based on clear, objective criteria.
2. The criteria must make sense to both customers and the sales team.

If you adhere to these two simple rules, you can pass the ultimate test and explain to one customer how and why another customer qualified for a lower price. Confidence in pricing allows sales professionals to justify differentiation in pricing without any of the pain and suffering that many salespeople go through when challenged why another customer is getting a lower price.

Can your customers see this logic in your offerings? If not, you are eroding their trust. You are also encouraging them to play poker with your sales teams and negotiate more vigorously. If customers don't see logic and integrity in the price-value trade-offs you ask them to make, your business is seriously underperforming relative to its potential. Think about it. Any measure that you choose to look at—net promoter score, customer longevity, lifetime value, net price realization, average order size—every one of them will suffer because of poor fences.

A company that worked this process well is Dow Corning. Dow Corning controls 40 percent of the global market for silicones, but in recent years they have been under relentless attack from low-priced competitors. Instead of commoditizing their products and services by responding directly, they created a low-value product, Xiameter. To avoid cannibalization of its premium offerings, Dow created a series of strong fences.

Figure 6.4 shows how the two offerings compare. The cheaper product has a narrower range of choices and considerably fewer services to accommodate the lower price. It also forces customers to make choices between value in exchange for lower prices. The results from this move were impressive. The company lost $28 million in the year before launching Xiameter and earned over $500 million in the year after the launch.[3]

Dow Corning	Xiameter
7000 Products	350 Products
Premium Price	20% Price Discount
Rapid Delivery	7–20 Day Delivery
Full Technical Service	No Technical Service
Custom Lot Sizes	Full Truck or Pallet Orders
International Terms	Limit to 6 Currencies

Figure 6.4 Uses of Fences to Manage High- and Low-Value Offerings.

The Final Piece: Bundling

A central goal of this rule was to recognize the power of tightening up your offering structure to improve the ability of your sales teams to manage tricky price negotiations. You've gotten to work on defining a low-value flanking offering. You're defining your core, expected, value-added levels of your offering. You're defining high-, medium-, and low-value services, and you are committed to getting fairly paid for them.

There are two challenges that still need to be addressed. The first is the recognition that most businesses sell offerings to different customer segments that place different value on these offerings. The second challenge is the recognition that, within segments, individual customers also value the same offerings differently. Without a well-thought-out plan for managing these two realities, a business's prices will naturally drift downward to accommodate the most price-sensitive customers. To be sure, accepting this downward drift is one way to ensure a business is covering its entire market. But it certainly is not the most profitable approach, as it leaves money on the table with those customers that value and are willing to pay more for your offerings.

The way to solve this problem is to use bundles. The logic of bundling is straightforward. The idea is to package two or more products, services, or attributes to create fixed-price variable-value packages. This is done in order to:

1. Get customers to buy more than they ordinarily would by offering a financial incentive—a bundled price—that is lower than

the sum of the component prices. The key here is to make the savings on the bundle attractive enough that customers will buy the bundle.

2. Create opportunities to earn more for your value when you have groups of customers that place different levels of value on the individual components of a potential bundle.

Pricing to reach the whole market often means setting prices low enough that even those customers that value your offering the least would be willing to purchase it. It's the lowest common denominator approach. Bundling provides a means of getting more revenues from individual elements of the offering than if they were priced to reach the whole market. It allows you to serve those customers while still getting paid more from those customers that place a higher value on your offerings. Let's look at how this works.

Imagine that you are a product manager for a software company providing solutions for tracking customer usage and predicting future behaviors. You are currently focused on two markets. The first is intercity rail and bus travel. The second is casinos. You've interviewed a number of customers and gained some great insights.

Casinos place a higher value on the ability to track usage patterns of high rollers because it allows them to set triggers to provide complimentary services (comps) real time, while the high rollers are still on the floor of the casino. The goal, of course, is to keep these high-value customers gambling. The casinos value the ability to predict future spending behaviors of these high rollers so they can cultivate relationships with them.

On the other hand, passenger rail companies are interested in encouraging more people to take the train. With this focus, these companies place more value on use tracking as a means to coordinate simple promotional campaigns. They place some value on trend analysis, but only for some simple collaborative promotions that they perform for local hotels.

Figure 6.5 demonstrates the price sensitivity that two different types of customers have for two different software products. A gambling casino will be willing to pay $600 for use tracking software

	Use Tracking	Trend Analysis
Gambling Casino	$600	$1,200
Passenger Rail Company	$1,000	$400

Figure 6.5   Price Sensitivity.

but $1,200 for the trend analysis software, since it will help them determine how to "comp" their loyal customers. The passenger rail company has a higher value ($1,000) for the use tracking software but would only be willing to pay $400 for the trend analysis package. One question Figure 6.5 can help resolve is What should the individual prices be? Clearly, $1,000 for the use tracking software and $1,200 for the trend analysis piece will permit getting the highest value out of the market. If you want the whole market, prices will be lower and that's where bundling comes in to (a) help us capture the whole market and (b) do that without leaving a lot of money on the table.

Without bundling, if we want to price to cover the whole market we are forced to the lowest potential prices: $600 for use tracking and $400 for trend analysis. We would then be limited to collecting a maximum of $1,000 from customers in each segment ($600 + $400). The problem is that this solution leaves a lot of money on the table. After all, the passenger rail companies are willing to pay $1,000 for use tracking, and the gambling casinos are willing to pay $1,200 for trend analysis.

The way out of this predicament is to look at what each segment is willing to pay for *both* modules together. In this case, casinos are willing to pay $1,800 ($600 for use tracking and $1,200 for trend analysis). The passenger rail companies are willing to pay a total of $1,400 ($1,000 for use tracking and $400 for trend analysis). By looking at the problem this way, we see that we can charge $1,400 for a bundle consisting of use tracking and trend analysis. This is 40 percent more than if we don't use bundling.

The Nuts and Bolts of Bundling

Given how critical bundling is to the financial health of your organization, we need to spend more time laying the groundwork for lining up the objectives. A credible set of bundles is the result of following a straightforward process.

1. Start with a simple approach to customer segments. In Rule Two, "Understand Your Value to Your Customer," we talked about customer triggers of value. This is a great place to begin. A data provider that we worked with knew its data was of high value. It was selling tens of millions of dollars worth of information products every year. What it didn't know was how customers were actually using the data in their investment decision-making process.

   Customer research uncovered three different uses for the data. The majority of customers applied their own analytic processes to scroll down the universe of potential investments to select a reasonable subset for easier investing decisions. In addition, some customers wanted to alter the assumptions behind the data to create new portfolios for their own analysis. Still other customers used the data as a reality check against analysis and decisions their own advisors had performed—in other words, a risk mitigation technique.[4] This simple understanding of customer value provided the basis for the next step.

2. Develop relevant product and/or service bundles for segments with high to low values to accommodate behaviors. Many of the bundles currently in use do not pass the relevance test. When reviewing your own bundles, ask a simple question. Are these items bundled together because they logically go together in the minds of your salespeople and customers, or because you hope that by putting them together you can create some sort of black magic alchemy that will miraculously make customers want to

spend large sums of money with you? If it is the latter, customers will not be fooled by bundling offerings that are not relevant to their needs.

The data provider used their understanding of what customers value to create offerings with data and some analytic tools. To drive this strategy, it created a basic platform to enable control of functionality and access to the data. Since most customers initially used the data for screening, this basic functionality was provided to every customer. More advanced screening techniques could be added and paid for if customers so chose. Other functionality, such as making adjustments to the underlying analysis behind the data, was another add-on. By limiting access to data through functionality and charging specifically for what the client needed, the data provider fenced off high-value functionality, thus protecting the price.

3. Price individual items higher than combined bundles. Without individual component prices that are higher than the bundled price, there is no incentive to buy the bundle. The discount doesn't need to be large, something on the order of 10 to 15 percent can be quite effective.

Don't Bungle the Bundle!

Bundling of products and services works. It simplifies the purchase and causes customers to buy more products or services. The bundle price, of course, has to be lower than the combined prices of the components. Once the price of any of the individual products gets to a certain level, the logic for the bundle is destroyed, as is any incentive to buy the bundle. Individual product prices continually need to be rationalized with the prices of all bundles in which they are included, even during short-term or end-of-month promotions. That is the way you protect the integrity of the bundle.

This is the point that most managers miss. If you adopt lower prices for the individual components, your customers will be able to break the bundle by buying individual components for a lower total price. In addition to allowing the prices of the individual components of the bundle to be too low, there are two other ways that managers typically "bungle the bundle."

First, they force customers to buy things that they don't value. This is a serious point of contention with some customers of enterprise software. Many have become very sophisticated in the management of these complex systems. They rely on highly trained internal staff and typically use older, more stable versions of the software. Yet they are often forced to buy maintenance packages that are focused on driving upgrades and delivering fixes to current versions. Instead of offering support packages for these sophisticated but slower-moving customers, software suppliers try to force them to upgrade or drop their maintenance contracts.

Increasingly, such customers are doing just that and turning to third-party support organizations that will meet their needs. Given that up to 80 percent of software firm revenues come from maintenance, support, training, and consulting, this certainly appears to be a short-sighted decision by the software suppliers.

Another way to undermine your bundles is to allow customers to break the bundle during price negotiations. We know of a supplier of industrial components that offered discounts based on the number of items on an order and total dollar volume: a legitimate form of bundling for large accounts. Poker-playing customers would then try to cherry-pick the individual items that appeared to have the best individual prices from our client and give the rest of the business to competitors. The client let them do this out of fear of losing all of the business. The end result was that the incentives used to encourage placing the entire order with our client were gutted and street prices on the individual items fell precipitously, eventually causing the company to be sold to a competitor.

What they should have done was to show percentage discounts for the total piece of business and not let the customer place orders with the lower prices. The discounts should have been earned and granted *after* the volume met the required levels. Yes, it would have taken some backbone in the selling process to accomplish this—that's in Rule 8!

Final Thoughts

Your product and service offerings are your most underutilized assets in building pricing confidence. If they are haphazardly allowed to evolve, key offerings lose definition. They also lose their unique value propositions. Confusion reigns, your pricing suffers, and you diminish the returns on your investments in development and innovation.

Organizations that have gotten over this hurdle do some things that are distinctly different. They are rigorous about connecting their insights about customer value to tightly defined offerings. They use combinations of products, services, and solutions to create price levers for their sales teams to control negotiations. They also know that there is no distinction between their pricing models and price lists and their offering structure. Offering architecture defines the possibilities and limits of what can be done in pricing. The first reaction of many executives, after coming to this realization, is that lack of this connection means that most of their offerings are undervalued by customers, and that a significant number do not have a sustainable position in the market. What about yours?

Notes

1. James C. Anderson and James A. Narus, "Capturing the Value of Supplementary Services," *Harvard Business Review*, January–February 1995.
2. Theodore Levitt, "Marketing Success Through Differentiation—of Anything," *Harvard Business Review*, January–February 1980.
3. Nirmalya Kumar, "Strategies to Fight Low-Cost Rivals," *Harvard Business Review*, December 2006.
4. Harry M. Lawson and Rachel Jacobsen, "Divide and Conquer: Product and Price Strategies for Data Service Companies," *Holden Advisors Whitepaper*, September 2006.

FORCE YOUR COMPETITOR TO REACT TO YOUR PRICING

Every player enjoys one or more value advantages. The trick is to use your value to stop leaving money on the table. Smart players know they don't have to participate in a competitive pricing death spiral. They map their markets. They define where they do and do not have a value advantage over their competitors. They know where and how to compete on price. Most important, they know where and how not to.

C ompetitors are a necessary evil in business today. It makes doing business more difficult. But, if we're honest, we will acknowledge that the competition is good for markets. It helps keep the focus on innovation, efficiency, and value. The problem most of us have with competitors is our attitude. We vilify the competition. *We* compete fairly; *they* cheat. We conclude that they are either fiendishly clever or behaving irrationally. We spend inordinate amounts of energy reacting to competitors. We choose to regard ourselves as victims. Somehow we rarely consider that competitors think about us precisely the same way we think about them.

Our attitude about competition justifies much of our destructive behavior, such as rampant price discounting. Attitude causes us to pull the price trigger too often. It causes us to get into negotiations that we should walk away from. Our attitude causes us to lose pricing power. We need to change the attitude of powerlessness and replace it with one of confidence. The best advice we can offer is more than 3,000 years old. "The best general enters the mind of his enemy," wrote Lao Tzu in the *Tao Te Ching*. To be more successful in our markets and with our customers, we need to do a better job understanding our competitors. We need to understand what they are doing, what their next move may be, why they are likely to make that move, and what they are likely to do in the future.

The trick when you are dealing with competitors is not to react to them. They are probably attacking in a place where you have a lot to lose and they have a lot to gain. Instead, get competitors to react in a region or with a customer where they have the most to lose and you have the most to gain. That way you are less likely to get hurt. Also, it is less likely there will be a damaging price war. To get there takes a system of understanding and responding properly to competitors; whether by matching price or making a public announcement, the intent is to minimize the damage of price competition.

Intuit, one of the Ten Most Admired Companies in *Fortune* magazine's 2007 survey, develops personal finance and tax software. We talked about how effective their offering is in Rule Six. The Mountain View, California–based company continues to dominate its markets despite the fact that mighty Microsoft, among many other players, has been a competitor for years. Microsoft even made a failed bid to buy Intuit in the 1990s. Microsoft is twenty times the size of Intuit and has plenty of cash to go after Intuit's lucrative markets. Yet Intuit stays ahead by relentlessly understanding its customers' needs. It does a great job of introducing low-cost, entry-level products. It does a great job of customer service. It has good relationships with the 200,000 accountants who are key buying influences. Intuit also spends a lot of time anticipating what Microsoft and its other competitors will do next. It tries to make sure its own development resources are focused in the most desirable areas. Intuit realizes that Microsoft will continue to target the small business accounting market. It has developed a number of scenarios on the potential impact Microsoft can make. This intelligence allows Intuit to keep developing and preannouncing new products that keeps Microsoft off-balance. It uses nimbleness as an advantage. Intuit has entered the mind of its enemy and has prospered.

Intuit doesn't just react to Microsoft; it stays ahead of Microsoft. If Intuit went head-to-head with Microsoft, it would lose. The goal is to keep Microsoft in catch-up mode. And they do it not with price but with relentless innovations of their products and services. Nimbleness and innovation limit Microsoft's ability to use price to elbow its way into the market. That's the trick in dealing with competitors. And it's a great example of how to use product and service innovations to stay ahead of competitors you can't beat in a price-driven conflict. If you do have to use price to deal with competitors, don't react to their moves. Think about ways to get them to react to you instead. When action is taken, make sure it is not a reaction but a well thought through game plan that will focus not on beating competitors but on getting them off your back. That's an important difference. PeopleSoft and Oracle tried to beat each other. They both gave massive discounts to customers who adopted their high-value enterprise software, but they both left lots of money on the table. PeopleSoft eventually lost the battle when it was acquired by Oracle. Now Oracle is going after SAP. SAP is much larger, and is reacting not with lower prices but with better products *and* services. Now that's smart.

The Problem of Market Elasticity

When thinking about developing a competitive strategy, it is vital to start with customers. Some customers will switch their suppliers, often due to price, but they don't change their volumes. This is one of the actions that gets in the way of using price as a competitive weapon in mature markets. It results in price wars where the only winner is the customer. Customers make it look like they are willing to switch for a lower price, but they don't actually buy any more products. Remember the discussion of derived demand in Rule Three, "Apply One of Three Simple Pricing Strategies"? When competitors keep lowering price to accommodate the willingness of customers to switch, they reduce their revenue and, in many cases, eliminate any profits. The problem is that many managers confuse that activity for market elasticity, where markets actually grow as a result of the lower prices. In this case the customer did not offer the vendors any additional volume. They offered nothing in return for the lower price.

When employing a discount, the payoff should be to get something of value for the concession: a give-get. Any other use of a discount just reduces revenue and often eliminates profits. Sure, sometimes a company drops prices to close an order. But when it does, two adverse things invariably result. First, customers negotiate even harder next time. Second, the company leaves money on the table. So, before using price discounts, consider whether customers are actually going to buy more of your products or services. If not, the company may be better off not discounting and relying on better selling of tangible value. In this case, it should create trusses for more backbone in the selling process (see Rule Eight, "Build Selling Backbone").

As we've already talked about, price elasticity research attempts to determine a market's responsiveness to changes in price. It's not enough for a company to do price elasticity research on behalf of its own products. Unless the company also considers its competitors' response to a deal or market, it is missing a vital element of the analysis. Even if a market is elastic, when a competitor matches your price discount, it negates any market effect. If the market is inelastic, as most business-to-business segments are, the profit potential will be wasted.

So what is a manager with pricing responsibility to do? First, understand the demand elasticity of your customers. Second, understand the customer negotiating strategy. Third, learn and understand the competitors' strategies. Without careful consideration, any one of those strategies can negate a good plan of action.

A Pricer's Dilemma: Learning the Pain of Decreasing Price in a Mature Market

A useful way to think about the problem is with the analogy of the *prisoner's dilemma*. We call ours the *Pricer's Dilemma*. Using a modified version of the results grid, based on one developed earlier by Professor Richard Harmer when he was at Boston University, the Pricer's Dilemma is an iterative game played between two teams of managers. We often use it to train managers how to think about pricing in a mature market and the importance of how to communicate to the market along the way.

We break managers into teams, and each team competes with another team in a chosen industry. Each team is required to make a pricing decision for a number of rounds. The decision is to sell a product for a high or a low price. It's as simple as that. The teams have to make these decisions through a number of rounds of game play. The team that earns the most money in the end is declared the winner. But the results are often surprising and always brutal. See the results grid in Figure 7.1.

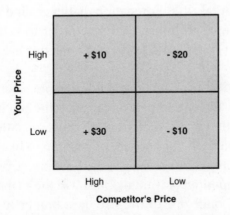

Figure 7.1   The Pricer's Dilemma: Pricing Competition in a Mature Market.

Most managers, after looking at Figure 7.1, conclude that the way to maximize profits is by reducing the price. A price reduction yields $30 profit. For this to happen, however, the competitor needs to keep its price high. If that happens in the first period of the game, the competing team would lose $20. They would be foolish to keep their price high for the next round (though we actually do see that happening), since it rewards the competitor's low prices. They need to match the low price, and quickly. Doing so puts both teams in a position where they each lose $10 per round.

We often see managers who play this game get frustrated because they want to adopt a value approach and keep their prices high. But a smart competitor will win the game by keeping their prices low. That's one of the training objectives: to get managers to recognize that if they do that, they can lose to the smart competitor. Value-based pricing is about more than keeping prices high; it's also about learning to deal with competitors who want to use low price to gain market share from you.

We also see a lot of opportunistic behavior. A team will price high for one round and then reduce prices for the next round. This strategy often occurs if the teams know the end of the game is imminent. But in long-term play, the results of opportunism are the same: Both competitors price low and lose money. The only way to make money playing the game is to have both competitors keep their prices high. That takes determination, patience, and a willingness to avoid short-term opportunistic gains in order to achieve long-term market stability. That should be the real objective in a mature market: market stability.

The bottom line in mature markets is that price competition really makes no sense. Every competitor can play the pricing game and is likely to do so if it doesn't think through the implications. Customers who came to you for low prices are now going to be the first to leave when a competitor offers lower prices. Low prices provide the least sustainable competitive advantage. Just ask the managers of AT&T. In 2004, AT&T, once one of the strongest brands in the world, saw close to a 50 percent decline in profitability as cost-effective regional competitors hammered them with still lower prices. Despite offering lower prices, AT&T continued to lose customers to other service providers. Though there were many reasons, price competition in a mature market was probably one of the most important elements in the downfall of the once mighty AT&T.

To compete successfully in mature markets, avoid price competition when you can, but be willing to let competitors know that you'll match their low prices if necessary. This is a lot like nuclear proliferation. You've got to have your own nukes as a deterrent to keep others from using theirs. But the doctrine of mutual assured destruction is a doctrine that has value only if it is never invoked. There's a lot of saber rattling and brinksmanship along the way. The intention of both the weapons and the blustering is to keep others from using their weapons. The doctrine worked with nuclear weapons, and it works with pricing.

Another way to successfully compete is to identify and quantify value drivers you can improve on with customers and make them the focus of your new product and service development. This is what AMD has chosen to do in the PC microprocessor business. AMD has gained both profits and market share by avoiding price competition rather than encouraging it. Instead, they focus on leveraging their outstanding technical skills by introducing the first 64-bit processor two years ahead of Intel. Unfortunately, as both AMD and Intel have discovered, some level of price competition is inevitable when inventories bulge and large customers demand it. One goal is to develop systems that anticipate what competitors might do and try to mitigate the damage of those competitive moves as much as possible.

Developing a Competitive Information System

When markets mature, they become less responsive to changes in price. Yet customers get more sophisticated in how they encourage suppliers to pull the low price lever. And, there are competitors that are willing to respond. The net result is that industry and company profits take a nosedive. When this happens or when it is apparent that it will happen in the not-too-distant future, it is wise to adopt systems that develop better responses to customer and competitive price pressures. Developing selling backbone solves one problem; developing a competitive information system solves the other.

These systems are intended to make sure that when you do make a move, it doesn't lead to unanticipated problems. Those moves can be actions such as match a competitor's price, respond to an RFP, make a public pricing announcement, or take a pricing action with a customer or in a market. The problems can include misinterpretation of a competitor's action that leads to the continuation rather than the cessation of a price war. This can cause customers to trust less and put the vendor through the pricing meat grinder.

Marketers assume competition is the villain when they hear about a lower price from a customer. We've seen many cases where the real villain is the company itself. It floats prices in the market without controls or records, or it responds to a price spilled from one market segment to another. In the end they are just competing with themselves. Or, the company just panics and responds to the games that purchasing agents play.

The competitive system doesn't have to be complicated or consume lots of resources. It does have to be process-driven and complete, if it is going to be effective. The process is intended to make sure that everyone in the company is cooperating and is presenting a united front rather than acting like rogue cowboys in the wild west. There are six steps to this process for better decision making (see Figure 7.2).

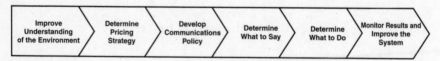

Figure 7.2 Competitive Information System.

Take the Six Steps

Step 1. Improve Understanding of the Environment

The objective here is to make sure the people making the decisions have a good understanding of the current competitive environment. Included is information like primary competitors, their financial situation, their historical and anticipated competitive strategy, and their position at your important and target customers. Understand market conditions, including growth cycles, expected short-term growth, and so on. Understand account level information, such as which competitors are active at your different accounts and which competitors are winning RFPs. Scan press announcements and interviews coming out of different competitors. Look for indications that they are changing their strategy. A good database of competitive information can draw a better picture of what is really going on in a particular market and with a particular customer. Someone does need to be responsible and continually update this database so managers will be more likely to use it in routine decision making.

A number of years ago, we were preparing an analysis of a market oligopoly (two competitors) that had a history of brutal price competition. This price competition was caused by intermediaries and actually encouraged by the two suppliers because they thought it helped their sales. We found that the intermediaries of one firm had been making public announcements concerning the aggressive price competition that was occurring in the channel. The intermediaries of the other side, lacking any systematic process or collection point to hear what their competitors were saying, were not able to effectively respond and stabilize the prices. The net result is that they *both* left a lot of money on the table. Make sure you understand the ability of a competitor to actually implement whatever strategy and tactics it is announcing; many times it just can't.

Step 2. Determine Pricing Strategy

Make sure the global pricing strategy can be implemented in local countries. Remember, there are only three pricing strategies: skim, penetration, and neutral. For any product and its spot in its life cycle, the strategy will evolve, and the key is to know the market timing to adjust proactively. On a global basis, that strategy will change to reflect local market conditions. Given that strategy, allocate discounts at a local level to achieve specific market objectives. This should be based on the analysis discussed in Rule Three, "Apply One of Three Simple Pricing Strategies." The important element is to have control over whatever strategy is chosen. Importantly, have the discipline to stick to that approach at all levels of the organization. It doesn't do any good to have a pricing strategy and then have a senior executive panic with the price lever.

Step 3. Develop Communications Policy

Communicating to the marketplace is important and can help avoid price wars. To be successful, companies need to have policies that control what people say to anyone outside of the company. Even casual comments to the salesperson of a competitor at the local gym can be misconstrued at best and can be illegal at worst. Companies that lack internal policies are at risk of sending signals that can actually continue price wars. Further, when employees do communicate with competitors in a manner that is unlawful, companies that don't have effective policies and training can find themselves liable for treble the damages.

The policy should identify primary spokespeople to represent the division and the entire company, when it comes to externally representing the positioning on competitive and pricing activities. Effective spokespeople are often the CEO, CFO, or EVP of sales and marketing. Whoever is identified, support them with coaching, best done by an outside professional, on what to say and how to say it. The press often looks for soundbites that will make a story better. Well-trained spokespeople know how to make and stick to their point so that it doesn't get lost in the clutter of other questions.

At the same time, the policy must explicitly identify the spokespeople for the company, identify who is *not* to say things to the press, and identify a clearinghouse for all press inquiries. All employees should be trained on those policies. This way, when any employee is contacted, he or she knows how to refer the reporter to the right people. And, if it's directly by a competitor, the employee knows enough to quickly terminate the discussion and report the event to the legal department.

This is what NUCOR Steel does with great effect. At a recent industry meeting, several of the competitors started talking about price, and the NUCOR manager turned his empty glass over and walked out of the meeting. By doing so, the NUCOR manager saved his company a lot of legal headaches but he had to be trained to do that. Finally, the proper people should respond to a competitor's message when it hits the press. The faster the company responds, the more likely their messages can have an impact in the market.

Step 4. Determine What to Say

Given what you know about the market, the competitors, and your own ability to execute a strategy, you need to determine what the right thing is to announce to a market. The trick here is to recognize that what you say can set the standard of performance for customers and competitors in an industry. We see many companies announce they are going to compete on value. Yet, their salespeople and managers have not yet broken from the habit of using price discounts to meet sales objectives. Thus not only do they leave money on the table, their customers perceive them as hypocrites. It's important to recognize that unless the systems and the discipline are in place to back up the strategy, having a program like this can undermine the goals of the company. A number of considerations need to be talked about in this situation.

What is the pricing strategy? This is especially true if it has been decided not to use price as a competitive weapon, be it a skim or neutral pricing strategy. Announcing the commitment to compete on value sends a signal to all competitors that the price weapon has been sheathed. On the other hand, do not talk about having a penetration pricing strategy because by delaying the time it takes competitors to actually see it, the better it will be for you. Announcing the willingness to *use* a low price strategy, along with the hope that you won't, sends a clear signal to the market that you are looking to stabilize the competitive environment.

If the company has a cost position that gives it an edge to compete better than others, it's actually a good idea to announce it to the market. Doing so will often lessen the likelihood of a competitor responding. The trick here is to use a public announcement to either warn off a competitor or get them to see the vision of a stable competitive environment. A number of years ago, Herb Kelleher, CEO of Southwest Airlines, announced that Southwest had taken out options on 10 Boeing 767 aircraft. The 767 is a long-haul, cross-country carrier and quite inconsistent with Southwest's strategy of flying only Boeing 737s. When a reporter asked why they were doing this, Kelleher responded that they were concerned about competitors coming after them in their West Coast markets and they wanted to be ready to respond, if needed. By making the announcement, Kelleher sent a strong signal to United Airlines and other legacy carriers that he was prepared to attack them in their long-haul markets, but hoped he didn't have to. As a result of that announcement, United pulled back on its discounting in West Coast markets.

It's a good idea to communicate if a company is willing to respond aggressively to a competitor that decided to attack using price. We often see companies send mixed messages in this area. If a company says that they are going to protect share in a mature market, it will probably accomplish only half its purpose. That message says that if a competitor comes after them, they are going to go after the competitor. Protecting share fails to deal with the real objective: a stable competitive environment. A better approach is to talk about the concern for the industry and the company's willingness to respond *if necessary*. This sends a more balanced message.

Step 5. Determine What to Do

The corporation needs to back up what it says with its practices. We often see companies publicly communicate their pricing intentions in the market and then do something completely different. The telecommunication companies did this coming out of the 2000 downturn. While trying to get out of the price wars with public announcements, they continued to win deals at any price with predictable results: low profits and consolidation in the industry. Also, failure to stand behind public communications just exacerbates price competitive behavior in an industry. So, it's important to resist temptation for opportunistic behavior and develop a program that puts discipline in whatever policies are developed. Salespeople need to be trained on the new policies, and senior managers need to know that they have to stick with the guidelines, too.

It's great fun to use a competitor's tactics against them. If they are coming after some of your customers, rather than respond to them through your own customers, go to *their* big customers and let them know that other customers are perhaps getting lower prices than they get. This type of exercise can quickly short-circuit a competitor's opportunistic behavior. If not, and you want to keep the business with a current account, you can offer a *five-minute price*. That is, you can offer the price verbally to the customer and let them know if they don't accept it in five minutes the price will no longer be effective.

If you don't really want to get that order, just give the competitor a chance to respond to it. When the competitor sees that their pricing moves with your customers are going to lead to price discounting for their existing customers, it makes them much less likely to use price against you. To accomplish this, it takes a good understanding of all of the significant customers in a geographic market and their primary supplier. This is not difficult to do, and it builds the capabilities of the firm to moderate price moves of a competitor. Price competition is like a game of chess where multiple moves determine the outcome.

Step 6. Monitor Results and Improve the System

Anyone who expects the system to be perfect at the start is in for a rude awakening. The companies that are successful at this, such as Caterpillar and Intel, started the process a long time ago, made their mistakes, and improved the system to the point that today they are competitive powerhouses in their respective industries. The key element of this step is to make sure there is focus outside of the business to continuously assess what competitors are saying and doing with their products and price. It's especially important to look at organizational changes that may impact the development and execution of pricing strategy. A new CEO, a desperate sales VP, the loss of a key customer can each impact what a competitor does in its own special way. At the same time, monitor the results of what your own organization is doing. The key here is consistency of the message and a direct link between the message and the execution. Don't worry about getting it perfect each time, just worry about getting it going.

Too many managers complain about the irrational behavior of competitors. Instead, they should worry about developing systems to control those behaviors. Companies can use those systems to anticipate competitors that may be causing some of the profit problems in an industry. Industries that have a lot at stake because of their massive investment in R&D as well as plants tend to be better at developing such systems. The chemicals industry is a great example. DuPont and Dow Chemical have developed state-of-the-art processes that give them the ability to manage competitive information and use the inputs to this process to effectively manage their own capacity, costs, market positions, and pricing. Each firm effectively communicates its intents and expectations of business capabilities and performance for the benefit of themselves and the industry as a whole.

Building the Global Chessboard

We were recently hired by a client for the purpose of training general managers and salespeople how to price with confidence. After the meeting, we met with salespeople to talk about how to deal with an anticipated slowdown in their industry. One salesperson was complaining about how recent price increases had caused problems for a customer in a particular industry segment and thought a price increase should be rolled back. After that meeting, one of the senior managers commented they really didn't want to be discounting in that particular industry segment anyway. The manager was tired of the salesperson complaining about problems with that customer. The salesperson had a loyal customer he was trying to protect. He was doing the *right* thing. The problem wasn't with the salesperson; he was doing his job. The problem was that the manager hadn't let the salesperson know the customer was in an industry segment the company had decided was not worth the discounts they required.

In the end, selling is a tactical job. Salespeople are in the trenches trying to land every deal they can. The job of managers is to tell salespeople who the desirable customers are and to warn the pricing people away from customers who cannot be served at a profit. Customers who cannot be served at a profit aren't bad people. They just cannot be served at a profit. At least not by your company. If such customers can be served at a profit by someone else, then everyone is better off. Of course, if that's the case, a useful question to ask is why Company B can serve such customers at a profit when Company A cannot. More to the point, if a customer cannot be served at a profit, it is in your best interest if your competitor has the honor of losing money on the relationship. In the case we just mentioned, the manager hadn't done that. He knew what were good and bad segments but failed to communicate this information to the salesperson. The net result was a frustrated manager and a frustrated salesperson.

In order to price with confidence, companies need to know they are targeting the right customers and the right segments. Strategy is required to do that. Strategy is required to help people meet their objectives. There is a very simple tool that can be used to communicate the direction that pricing people need to take with their discounts and salespeople need to take with their selling efforts. We call it the *discount grid*, or a chessboard. The reason we call it a chessboard is because it helps managers map their efforts to checkmate a competitor in a manner that is agreed on by the senior managers. It reduces conflict and anxiety and gets everyone working in the same direction with their time and discount resources.

Figure 7.3 is an example of the discount grid. The grid provides the backdrop understanding that is critical for effective competitive information management. It contains the information on what to say and what to do with pricing and selling efforts. In its simplest form, as shown here, it takes a firm's primary segments and customers (in this case based on size) and prioritizes them.

In this case, there are four simple priorities. Let's consider four segments called *current strong, grow, move product,* and *ignore.*

- In the *current strong* segments, the company has a strong market position and there is little it can do to extend its market position without causing a price war. The decision is to take care of this segment and defend if necessary.
- The *grow* segments receive the majority of the discounts. The company might be growing or it might be in an area where

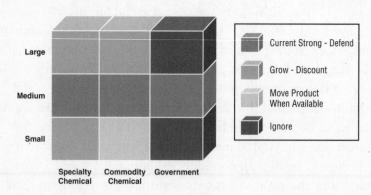

Figure 7.3 Global Discount Grid Chessboard.

competitors are stronger. So the intent is to grow penetration in that segment.

- The *move product* segments are the ones where the company can move product at very low prices without upsetting the competitive balance in the industry. It should be made up primarily of price buyers, attractive only when the company has a bunch of excess capacity.

- The *ignore* segments represent customers who may be served if they want to meet the price. But if they want a discount, forget about it!

Look at what this grid does for everyone in the company. It identifies, in a very simple manner where and how to deal with customers—all of them. It puts a stake in the ground for where to discount. Review Rule One, "Replace the Discounting Habit with a Little Arrogance," for details of this point. The grid shows managers where they should be spending their time and, maybe more important, where they shouldn't be spending their time. It can be put together fairly quickly by the leadership of the firm. And, it meets one of the primary requirements of leadership: providing people direction. If managers don't do this, they will not effectively deal with conflicting agendas in the silos within the company. Companies that do this tend to execute strategy much more precisely.

Successful companies have a good understanding of who their competitors are, what they are good at, and what they are bad at. Managers take those insights and instead of reacting directly to a competitor's moves, they determine strategically where and when to respond to those moves. And, they understand how to best respond in a way that doesn't turn the interaction into a customer or industry-level price war. When those insights and actions are turned into effective competitive information systems, they provide long-term competitive advantage that stops leaving money on the table in ineffective price battles with competitors.

BUILD YOUR SELLING BACKBONE

Teach Your Sales Force and Managers to Negotiate with Value

The best pricing strategy will fail unless salespeople and managers have backbone in the selling process and the ability to defend it. Confidence in negotiation requires confidence in pricing. Confidence in pricing comes from knowing the value of your products or services. It also comes from knowing your customer. Backbone comes from knowing the tricks your customers use to get you to drop price and how to deal with them.

The call came from one of our largest clients. The executive vice president of sales requested our help in a delicate sales negotiation with one of its most important customers. Our main expertise is in pricing, not sales negotiations, but this client insisted that he needed our help. So we cleared the decks and got to work. What follows is a detailed description of how a pricing strategy is determined, how it was defended, and how it turned out.

We reviewed what we knew about the situation. Our client is a semiconductor manufacturer working in a business that had at least half a dozen global competitors who manufactured a similar product. Thus we were dealing with a mature commodity in a highly price-sensitive market. We also learned that our client's customer—a well-known manufacturer of disk drives from the PC industry—needed the semiconductors to release its own product.

Our first step was to determine exactly what features the disk drive manufacturer required. We had our client send a team of technicians to visit the customer's design team. The client team came back with a five-page list of technical features that the disk drive manufacturer desired. Obviously, we were on a value hunt, looking for the specific opportunities in which our client could add value, differentiate its semiconductors, and price accordingly. Unfortunately, there were no value opportunities in the five-page list of technical features. All competitors had the same set of specifications.

We needed some information we could use to differentiate our client's product. We tried to set up formal meetings with our client's technicians and the customer's design team that was building the next generation of disk drives. At this point, the customer's purchasing agent became an obstacle, which is predictable behavior for a poker player. He wanted to control the relationship. But it's almost always possible to find another way. When formality fails, try informality. So at lunchtime, we had some of our client's technicians visit the customer with hot pizza and cold soft drinks.

Soon the conference room was filled with employees, including some from the disk drive design team. After a few of these lunches, our client's technicians were able to piece together some intelligence we could use. We learned that there were two preferred vendors: one was our client and the other was its largest competitor. That was good to know. Instead of having to beat six other competitors, we had to beat only one. We also learned that the customer had critical delivery requirements. This was a plus for our client, because it had a great track record for meeting delivery guarantees. Now we could get to work devising a specific pricing strategy.

We reviewed the numbers. Our client's semiconductor product was a $7.50 component that enabled the customer to ship a $300 disk drive. We assumed that the disk drive's gross margin was 30 percent, or $90. We made a number of other assumptions. We estimated that if the disk drive hit it big in the market, it would take three to six months for competitors to duplicate and ship a similar device. We calculated that the value the customer would derive by shipping a product with a $7.50 solution from our client was closer to $130. We further calculated that the competitor had a 95 percent chance of meeting the delivery requirements, and our client had a 100 percent chance. We concluded that the incremental value to the customer from choosing our client's product rather than the competitor's came down to $4 per unit. What's more, we believed the customer knew it.

But we weren't done yet. Our client was in a competitive industry, and we had to make sure their pricing met the reasonableness test. There was a lot of discussion around what percentage of the $4 incremental value we calculated they could safely grab and still be fair to the customer. In the end we advised our client to charge an extra 25 percent, or an additional $1, for the $4 of value we believe existed because of their unrivaled history of shipping on time. In the end, we recommended that our client hold to a pricing strategy that offered its product and delivery commitment for $8.50 per unit.

But we knew we weren't done yet. We had to get the client's senior leadership to have confidence in the pricing strategy for this opportunity. We knew this wouldn't be easy, as the customer's purchasing manager would pull out all the stops in an attempt to negotiate a lower price.

The negotiations were classic. The customer's purchasing agent ripped our client's selling team up one side and down the other. He used most of the purchasing tactics in Larry Steinmetz's list of tricks we described in Rule One, "Replace the Discounting Habit with a Little Arrogance." The purchasing agent made the client's pricing team cool their heels. He canceled meetings. He bluffed. He telephoned the executives, all in an attempt to exploit weaknesses in our pricing strategy. But with training from us, the executives anticipated all his moves and wouldn't budge. At the end of the negotiations, the customer placed an order with our client for 100 percent of its semiconductor business for a price of $8.48 per device. A two cent per device gesture helped cement the order.

So our client was very happy, and it never had to play its trump card. It had confidence in the value of its product and rode that confidence to victory. But what if the purchasing agent had been a price buyer and demanded a price lower than $8.48 per device? That's when the trump card would be played. Our client would say, "We'll be pleased to meet that lower price, but at that price we cannot give you the delivery guarantees you expect." We understood that delivery to volume was the customer's value trigger. Once we understood that, the advantage was ours.

It turned out to be a win-win for everyone. The customer sold 13 million disk drives incorporating our client's semiconductors. This company became our client's most profitable customer overnight. By going on a value hunt and with a little negotiations planning, we grabbed an additional $12.5 million off the table. To conclude, there are two important things our client did to make this outcome happen. First, it put some backbone into the selling process; and second, it stopped acting like a commodity and acted like a solution.

It's Easy for You to Say

"It's easy for you to say," a VP of sales told us during a training session. "You're not out there trying to meet quota."

Even if that were true, and it's not—everyone has a quota—it wouldn't change our position. We learned a long time ago that we can't afford to get rattled by price-oriented clients. We learned a long time ago that if we don't have confidence in the value of our services to our clients, we have no business doing what we do. We know that if we don't understand how much value we're going to add to an engagement, we have no business making a presentation about how we are going to add value. We began to ask the tough questions at the start of an engagement and if a customer wasn't willing to answer them, we took a deep breath and invited them to go with another vendor. We believe that we're a good solution for our clients. We know we have to act on that confidence if we're going to be successful.

Customers want you to focus on how you are the same as your competitors to level the playing field on price. But you have to focus on how you are different, and feel confident about the services you provide to make your solution better. Understand how that difference provides a better solution to customers and start acting like you are a solution. Stop acting like a commodity vendor. Instead, take that understanding of how you create value, add a dash of arrogance, and build the confidence you need to be successful in today's tough world of customer negotiations. Make your customers respect you and want to do business with you. Put some backbone into your selling process.

The Selling Problem

Yes, we know it will be hard, but any time companies are willing to lower prices to close an order, they have already lost in their negotiations with customers. Any time you don't understand and properly leverage the value you create for customers, money is left on the table. Buyers know that and use all the tactics we talked about in Rule Four to get salespeople and managers to lower prices. It's a game to customers.

The real problem is not with salespeople. It is managers and the compensation systems that force salespeople to bow to poker players. It's the *end-of-period desperation* that causes this senseless focus on price. It's the White Horse Syndrome where managers want to be heroes. Even in cases where managers have moved to profit-based compensation systems for salespeople, it often doesn't work well. This is because salespeople will still lower prices to close the big orders.

So let's consider the options for making changes. The first step is a little like a 12-step program. First we have to admit there is a problem. The second step is to recognize that salespeople and managers need to understand and focus on the value that they provide their customers. They have a right to charge for that value, and they should be confident in the price they set for a deal. The third step is to implement programs in the selling organizations to accomplish this move to value on a consistent and systematic basis. We call that *putting backbone* in the selling process.

Our goal is to get managers to view selling time as a scarce resource that needs to be used as effectively and efficiently as possible. When salespeople are poorly trained, have ill-fitting customer solutions, are compensated strictly on volume, and/or are constantly pushed to close a deal at the end of a quarter, the techniques of good selling and negotiation management fade into the background. As a result, even if the company makes their revenue numbers, they almost never make their profit numbers, unless there is diligent cost cutting. There is a limited time frame for negotiations. If you don't want to leave money on the table, prepare your salespeople and managers for account negotiations. You may be doing this, but we would suggest that you add a few more elements to that process to be more successful.

Prepare for Tough Negotiations

It takes planning to avoid leaving money on the table. Planning helps salespeople be better prepared for the tough questions and requests from ever more demanding clients. Make sure senior executives in the selling organization are included in the planning and are in agreement with the approach. Their involvement provides a level of assurance to everyone else that they won't undermine the negotiation as it moves forward. Finally, planning increases the likelihood of success no matter what account-level strategy and approach has been adopted. The more you plan, the greater the likelihood you will win the deal at a higher, more profitable price. We're not saying that high levels of planning are necessary with *all* accounts. There are many accounts in many business situations where the revenue and opportunity are small enough so it isn't worth the effort. The sales call may be more than enough to connect with the right people and provide the customer buying center with the information they need to make the decision. Some level of call planning is good discipline, but there are already plenty of basic sales tools and approaches that accomplish this. The type of account planning we're presenting here is designed as an additional set of techniques for the complex sale with larger accounts to protect your price and value along the way.

For salespeople and teams who are used to doing this type of work, it could be a one-hour planning meeting. For larger and more complex sales, it could take a number of planning sessions occurring over several months. This process forces the team to ask questions they aren't used to asking to get the right information to make informed decisions.

Here's the payoff. First, it ensures that you are doing your best to identify and meet the needs of the customer. Second, it provides you with an understanding of the financial implications of your solutions in comparison to those of your competitors for that particular customer's environment. Third, it makes sure that you are dealing with *all* individuals in the customer buying center. And by asking them the right questions, you assess their value drivers, power, and control in the process. Finally, it makes sure that you anticipate two critical reactions: that of the customer and that of the competitor. This way you have a secondary approach planned, rather than having to make it up in the heat of the negotiations. The bottom line is that preparation increases the likelihood of avoiding the commodity trap and having a better long-term outcome in the account, that is, profitable sales growth.

Account planning forces the connection of people in different functions within the selling organization. This means that they not only understand each others' position but they are working to improve the overall performance of the company with the customer.

The difference here versus the siloed organization is that they're communicating as a team on real business issues rather than talking past each other. (Siloed organizations do not interact within themselves or with other organizations.) They are centered on the needs of the customer. They are all focusing on making sure that when they improve their own performance, they can demonstrate the value of the improvements and earn a better price.

Step 1: Conduct Value Analysis

The objective is to link the customer value needs with what the company offers. Customer-level value analysis ensures that the products and services you offer have value and are positioned in a way to reflect that value. Too many times, sales teams and senior executives present useless rhetoric and features to customers. This undermines the credibility of the team with the customer. Step 1 is used to make sure the company performs in ways that create value and presents or discusses those things to customers in a manner that highlights tangible value.

We have seen many cases where a simple value exercise uncovers so much value that lots of additional research is not needed. We had one case where a 45-minute value discussion uncovered over $10,000 worth of value for a product that was priced way under $500. After we stopped laughing (to prove an important point), we used the exercise to identify which customers were most likely to appreciate that value and used those insights to begin focusing sales efforts on high-value accounts.

First, list all the products, services, and activities that the company offers the customer. Include product features, service features, technical support, design, customer service, special terms, or delivery, to name a few. Take a look at catalog sheets and advertising. List the things the company says in them as value drivers. If they talk about safety, list it. If they talk about quality, list it. The more the better.

Second, identify the primary competitors. Include both the good ones and the bad ones. Don't kid yourself on this one. If you don't know who your competitors are, go ask your customer. The purchasing agent might not tell you, but the technical or production people probably will.

Third, evaluate the performance of each competitor. This can be done qualitatively or quantitatively. If it is done qualitatively, use a simple scoring system to summarize the important value drivers and their approximate financial benefits. Drill down on how your offerings drive financial value for your customer. If you don't have the answers, ask the customer. Ask them how important services like delivery and technical support are to them. Ask what keeps them up at night and ask how you might be able to help.

Step 2: Conduct Buying Center Analysis

Purchasing in most organizations is not an event; it is a process. That process occurs over time. It involves a wide range of individuals. Each individual has different criteria for a vendor selection. The objective of this phase is to identify the individuals involved, the positions they hold, what their criteria are, and how much power and control they have over the process. A useful list of the functions that individuals can fulfill was developed by Professor Thomas Bonoma of the Harvard Business School:[1]

1. The *buyer* is the actual purchaser of the product. Buyers conduct the process of final purchase with the vendor. Depending on the type of product and its stage in the buying process, different individuals can be the buyer. In early stages of a new product or service's qualification, it can be a technical or production person. Once the buying becomes routine, the buying function tends to move over toward the purchasing agent.
2. The *gatekeeper* handles vendor contacts and controls the flow of information and contact with other members of the buying

center. The gatekeeper tends to be the purchasing agent. But in early phases of product or service selection, the gatekeeper can be a mid-level manager in the customer organization. The gatekeeper's primary job is to protect other members of the buying center, especially the decision maker, from vendor contact.

3. The *initiator* determines that a product or service is needed. This can be virtually anyone in an organization. For services, it can be a higher-level manager. For products, it can be a technical, maintenance, service person, or an actual user. For more routine purchases, the initiator can be an automated process which determines when stock levels are low.

4. The *influencer* is anyone who can influence the decision process, criteria, or outcome. Many different types of people can actually influence a decision. This is why it is important to map everyone involved in the process. If you fail to identify an influencer who has a level of power in the process and that influencer has a prior relationship with a competitor, that's almost always a danger signal that you've got some work to do to get a favorable outcome.

5. *Users* are the people who actually use the product. It's usually a good idea to check in with the people who use your products and services to find out their levels of satisfaction. If they are using a competitive product, ask them how they would like to see it improved.

6. *Deciders* are the actual decision makers. They are also known as "foxes," since they often try to hide from outside vendors, usually because their time is valuable and they want to offload this work onto their staff. Tough questions to any of the other individuals will either identify who the deciders are or actually get you a meeting with them to answer the tough questions. We've seen far too many deals lost because the team failed to see the shift in power from one individual to another. That's because they didn't ask the right questions throughout the selling cycle.

The real trick in buying-center analysis is to use your analysis to determine the type of buyer a customer really is. For example, if you're dealing with a third-party consultant, they will almost always be a poker player. They are there to teach the customer how to play better poker. They are there to help the customer get more discounts for high-value products and services. Your job in buying-center analysis is to use your understanding of the participants and their power and control to make an informed judgment of their likely behavior. To do that, you need to identify all of the individuals involved in the buying center. Then prioritize. What are their individual criteria for a decision; in other words, what are their value needs?

You get this information through those depth interview techniques we just covered. Yes, everyone in the center has a different set of needs. That's why the next thing you do is assess their level of power and control over the process. How do you do that? You ask them. When you do that, it's important to remember that gatekeepers and third-party consultants always overstate their power in the process. By dealing with multiple "informants," you develop a much better sense of where the real control lies. Your ultimate objective is to find the fox along the way.

Recognize that a single individual can fulfill multiple positions in the buying center. For example, a purchasing agent will be both the buyer and the gatekeeper in many cases. As purchases become routine, buying centers get smaller and total control moves over to the purchasing agent.

There is one last point on buying centers. Expect them to change without any notice. Many salespeople get burned when that happens. Sometimes those changes happen when a new member suddenly enters the mix. No matter what buying-center position that member may fulfill, game-changing criteria and process can result.

We had a potential customer with whom we were going through a proposal process, when a new mid-level manager joined the negotiating team. He added a favored vendor to the mix. What did we do? We stopped the proposal process. And, we made a few suggestions for dealing with the decision makers that we knew the competitors would be unable to do. We talked about the need to connect their new pricing controls to a very diverse and untrained sales force and the need to have some backbone in the execution of the new strategy in the senior leadership team. We knew that the new competitor didn't think like that. The net result is that we met with the senior executives, identified the fox, met her criteria, and got the business.

Be especially careful if the buying-center changes are organizationally mandated as it often signals a significant change in the buying behavior of the account. We knew of a company that hired a new purchasing agent who had a lot of experience rattling the cages of suppliers and getting them to drop prices. Our estimate was that this was a bluff, and we coached our client's selling and leadership team on how to respond to the new tactics. Six months later, even though the buyer was still trying his tricks, the supplier hasn't had to drop prices.

Step 3: Evaluate the Likely Buying Behavior

Value and Relationship buyers are fairly easy to identify. They are more open and honest about their real needs. They'll tell you what they want if you ask the right questions. But remember that no matter how much we talk about value, not all customers are willing to pay for it. To make matters worse, those that don't want to pay for it fall into two categories. The first are the price buyers. These are the ones who don't want value. They only care about getting the lowest possible price. The second group are the poker players. They've got all sorts of tricks to get suppliers to tremble and cave in the middle of negotiations. The important issue here is to anticipate what their approach is going to be and be prepared with the right set of responses. If you don't get rattled, they will begin to respect you. You build pricing power along the way. Buying centers can and will exhibit a variety of behaviors. Technical teams want value, and purchasing agents want low price. Your job is to weigh the level of control of each faction and determine what their real behavior is likely to be.

Step 4: Determine Your Coverage Strategy

The objective here is to take your analysis of the customer's buying center and their likely purchasing approach and develop an account coverage strategy to increase the likelihood of success with the account. It is important to make sure the people identified in the buying center are covered by the right managers in the selling organization. You don't want to waste time calling on people who don't care and don't need to see representatives from the selling team. Price buyers actually don't need to see salespeople or senior managers. They prefer to use the phone.

Senior managers should be trained on the value sell as much as the salesperson. In fact, they can often send a strong signal of how negotiations will go by taking strong positions on the value provided and what your expectations are during the negotiations. Finally, the sales coordinator has the responsibility of making sure that all senior managers will support the account strategy and not fold in the middle of the negotiations.

Two outstanding companies that do this are Cisco and General Electric. Cisco used CEO John Chambers as the spokesperson for the new world Internet economy. Chambers spends a large percentage of his time with customers at the chief executive officer level. Jack Welch, former CEO of General Electric, made it a common practice to call on customers to ink a value-based deal.

Samsung went so far as to send the head of its chip division, Hwang Chang Gyu, to call on Steve Jobs to get Apple to adopt new Samsung technology flash memory chips in the latest iPod nano. It wasn't easy and despite significantly higher prices for the new technology, the size and battery life benefits along with multiple sales calls were enough to win the day. As Samsung has proved, a dogged focus on disciplined and customer-focused technological evolution can position new technologies for successful adoption, sometimes in big ways. Add to that a senior leadership team that is very involved in customer-facing activities in a positive value-oriented manner, and it will be a winner every time.

Step 5: Offering Development

The objective in this phase is to translate the value needs of the players in the buying center and your assessment of the buying behavior into a meaningful account-level offering strategy. The point is that you need to develop a high-level offering structure, which can be summarized into important key elements. If you're not dealing with a true price buyer, those key elements should be supported by a calculation that shows the financial benefit. That calculation should be supported by an analysis of the connection between the stated value drivers and the key elements of the offering.

The service and support discussion is even more important than the product one. Many products may become commodities but services don't. Those are the real differentiators. Make sure that you have identified the important services and included them in a high-value bundle. And, take them out of the low-value bundle. The pulling of services from the low-price bundle is the key to making the poker player say, "Hey, we need that." Or, maybe they'll say, "Hey, your competitors are willing to do that." If you've done your homework, you know whether it's true.

The price you determine needs to be vetted. Why do you think the price will work? What is your support for why the prices you have charged are reasonable? If they are higher than the competitors, why do you think you should be able to charge them? You need to have your answers ready because the fur will be flying during negotiations, and you might not have time to put together good answers.

Finally, what are the critical success factors for this negotiation? What do you have to do to really make this work? What might happen to blow the process up? What do you need to do to make sure that you are communicating your value proposition and support effectively? Do you need better references? There are a number of questions that have to be thought through and dealt with to assure that you will have the best possible result.

Step 6: Develop the Primary Negotiating Approach

At this point, you need to get a number of issues in line. What is the customer's likely behavior and how are you going to deal with that? What are the specific value messages and what ROI analysis do you have to quantify them? Where do you stand relative to your competitors?

The added question at this phase relates to possible *closers*. These are the things you can throw on the table to get the deal closed. They are typically things like the extra discount. The problem is that this continues the focus on price. Therefore, it might be a better idea to have some closers that are value-based. Extra training, services, engineering or design help, and payment terms are all things that can be used. Yes, sometimes you want to charge for those things but it's usually a good idea to have a closer to push the customer over the edge to place the order. Remember the opening story in this chapter? The customer used a two cent discount to push the customer to closure. Closers need to be kept in your back pocket and not thrown on the table too early.

The final step is to determine the walk-away price. This is the price that you decided was the price below which you shouldn't go. This is the price that assures you some level of reasonable profit. It's also the threshold of walking away. Everyone on the team must agree, or at least respect, the number prior to the negotiations. There can be no senior people panicking at the last moment and dropping the price. The entire firm's credibility is at stake. Buyers know this. Yes, it does take courage.

We know of one services company that adopted this approach in a dramatic way. At the price negotiation, the prospective customer insisted on a price that crossed the company's walk-away threshold. So, at a signal from the lead negotiator, the entire team got up and, without a word, left the meeting and the building. The team got in their vehicle and drove to the airport. They were at the gate, waiting to board their plane back to the home office, when the call came. The prospective customer caved. It sent a limo to pick up the negotiating team and inked the deal on favorable terms to both parties. Sometimes confidence calls for a little brinksmanship.

Step 7: Determine the Expected Customer Response

This is perhaps the toughest part. It requires a good understanding of the people in the customer's buying center. You will never know for sure, but you can work to anticipate where the customer will disagree on key points you are trying to make. For those anticipated points of disagreement, you need to have either anecdotal or quantitative support. The same preparation is needed for the questions that they might ask you. The tech people may ask about documentation. You might want to bring technical manuals or have them available online. The support people may want to know about your 24/7 help desk. Take a page from the Boy Scouts. Be prepared. In anticipating questions and points of disagreement, preparedness is your goal.

Who do you think their final preference will be for a supplier? If it's not you, you've got to be honest with yourself. Maybe it's a good time to pull out of the negotiations. Some members of the buying team might not want you to pull out, but if the person who writes the checks has a relationship with another vendor, you are probably wasting your time. This is the biggest mistake that you can make during this process. During your discovery process, you could find that a senior-level decision maker has a relationship with another company. Other members of the buying center convince you to keep going through the process because they supposedly like you. But when the decision is made, the senior person almost always wins the day.

It's a good idea to take the account team and split it in half. Have them spend an hour and answer each of the questions. This will force all of them to get involved and think through the customer process. It will also give the entire team, once it gets back together, the opportunity to compare and discuss how they came up with different answers to the questions.

Step 8: Develop a Secondary Negotiating Strategy

Your objective here is to prepare answers for both the customer response to your initial strategy and the competitor's response as well. What will you do if the competitor drops price? Can you provide good answers to the questions you expect? Do you have the technical capabilities to handle the calls to the Web and the customer service divisions if needed? Remember, preparation is what this process is all about. "Chance favors the prepared," as the motto goes.

What about RFPs?

At this point, it's worthwhile to spend a few moments talking about Requests for Proposal (RFPs). An RFP is often a sign that a customer is not a relationship buyer and is likely not going to be a value buyer, either. Especially if they don't have identified selection criteria, which provide higher-value suppliers a chance to win. That means that RFPs come, for the most part, from price buyers or poker players. Before we give you any prescription, please answer the following questions. What percentage of your RFPs do you win? You would be surprised at how many managers don't know! The next question is How much time do your people spend on responding to each RFP? If it's more than an hour and your close rate is low, you are wasting resources responding to RFPs.

Dominant vendors to an account respond to customer RFPs too often. This is especially true when the RFP indicates a shift in buying responsibility from a technical person or a user to the purchasing agent. This is also the case when there is a third-party consultant handling the bid process. These people take products and services delivered by primary vendors, develop bare-bones specifications, and put them out to bid with a wide range of suppliers, many of whom are low-value. The worst thing that a dominant incumbent can do is to respond to the RFP. When they do, they are either going to have to drop their price significantly to win the business or they are going to have to lose the bid to a low-value vendor. If this marks the customer's move from a value buyer to a price buyer, you need to have a low-value offering such as we talked about in Rule Four, "Play Better Poker with Customers." If the customer is becoming a poker player, not responding to the bid is an excellent way to call their bluff. The nice thing about this approach is that it undermines the buyer's credibility with the rest of the buying center. If you are going to lose the business anyway to price, you might as well do everything you can to maintain your credibility too. What about reverse auctions? A *reverse auction* (also called *procurement auction* or *e-auction*) is a tool used in business-to-business procurement. It is a type of auction in which the roles of the buyer and seller are reversed, with the primary objective to drive purchase prices downward. In an ordinary auction (also known as a *forward auction*), buyers compete to obtain a good or service. In a reverse auction, sellers compete to obtain business. Reverse auctions are favored by poker players, who decide to put their suppliers through the wringer over a period of hours or days with an online bidding process that shows how unnamed competitors respond to an RFP and gives the managers a chance to respond on a real-time basis. Why do buyers do this? Simple. They do it because it works. It drives prices lower.

Any time a seller responds to a bid or an RFP, they need to stop, ask questions, and get answers to a number of quite basic questions. They need to assess whether or not this is going to be a fair bid among equals or whether a potential customer is just conducting a fishing expedition. We recommend that companies get answers from prospects to a number of basic questions before they agree to participate in the process:

1. What specific business problem are you trying to solve?
2. Who and/or what does that involve?

3. What is the likely return if you fix the problem?
4. What are the criteria for selecting a vendor to help?
5. What is the process for selecting a vendor to help?
6. What is the final process for approval of the project?
7. Who is the final sign-off and what is that person's position?
8. Is there a budget approved?
9. What is it?
10. If there is no budget, what is your sense of what this should cost?

Our actual list is much longer than this, but this list gets to the general point. The result of asking these questions is that you often find that the people who put these bids together haven't put enough thought into them to assure you that they are serious about the request. Sometimes, it is a casual attempt to see how suppliers will respond with no real intent to purchase anything. Sometimes it is an attempt to float an idea and see how suppliers respond to them. Sure, they want to purchase something but they also want the suppliers to educate them along the way. That's okay if you have a good chance of winning a piece of business. But, if you don't, let the winner educate the customer. Or, make sure you get paid to do it.

The next time a buyer tries to tell you that you're a commodity, take a deep breath and tell him or her that if they want commodities, there are six other competitors in your business they can buy from. Talk about all the things you do to help them that add value to the things they do. Talk about the things your company does to improve the quality of your products and services to them. Talk about the things your company does for the industry.

We accept that this process is not easy to implement in the real world. It requires confidence in your value. It entails some risk. In other words, do you have the fortitude to act on the value that you offer? There is no easy answer to this question, but it must be asked repeatedly. Pricing leaders avoid this question only at the great cost of distancing themselves from those they serve. Pricing leaders will make mistakes from time to time, but in testing themselves with each sales and lost opportunity, they will find the strength they need to prevail. Finding this out is not for the faint of heart, but then again, neither is pricing.

Notes

1. Thomas Bonoma, "Major Sales, Who Really Does the Buying?" *Harvard Business Review*, May–June 1982.

TAKE SIMPLE STEPS TO MOVE FROM COST-PLUS TO VALUE-BASED PRICING

Value-based pricing is an ideal. It requires sophisticated internal skills and systems. The trick to value-based pricing is to evolve pricing as the discipline and skills of your people improve. Start gradually. There is nothing wrong with cost-plus pricing as long as it does a good job of leveraging the financial value you create for customers.

Confidence in pricing requires building on your current capabilities. At the beginning that often means taking small steps and revisiting them repeatedly until they become core skills. Once your core skills are in place, you can make progress more quickly as what was once difficult becomes second nature. This is the only way to build your organization's pricing confidence. Over the long run, the goal is to have prices reflect the value you create for your customers.

But if yours is like most organizations, your goal of setting a coherent pricing strategy to reflect the value you deliver may be stuck in a particular pricing model that will almost certainly frustrate your goal. Many companies have their pricing strategies invested in cost-plus pricing, which is the strategy of covering your costs plus a determined profit.

Even though most managers are familiar with cost-plus pricing, it may be useful to review the model's advantages and disadvantages. Here are some of the advantages of cost-plus pricing:

1. Easy to calculate.
2. Simple to administer.
3. Requires minimal information.
4. Tends to stabilize markets.
5. Protects supplier from unexpected cost increases.
6. Believable to salespeople and customers.

But there are also significant disadvantages to cost-plus pricing:

1. Ignores demand, image, and market positioning.
2. Favors historical accounting costs rather than replacement value.
3. Applies standard output level to allocate fixed costs.
4. Offers few incentives for efficiency, as costs are passed off to customers.
5. Ignores the role of customers and the value they derive.
6. Creates a competitive disadvantage using average costs (as discussed in Rule 5).

In Rule Nine, we argue that value-based pricing is often a path to a more confident pricing strategy that does not leave money on the table. In contrast to cost-plus pricing, which assigns a percent markup over costs, value-based pricing focuses on the price you believe customers are willing to pay, based on the benefits your business offers them. If you have clearly defined benefits that give you an advantage over your competitors, you can charge according to the value you offer customers. In other words, value-based pricing depends on the strength of the benefits that you can demonstrate you offer to customers. But, we also believe that this is an ideal that takes time to implement effectively, especially in medium to large firms.

This rule provides a road map to get there, breaking down the steps to the ultimate objective of value-based pricing. We favor an incremental approach. While this slow but steady approach is not as radical as full-speed-ahead transformation efforts, a steady progression will lead to confidence in pricing that is internalized throughout your organization and resistant to the pressures that tend to erode pricing confidence.

Organizations that price with confidence work at it continuously. They recognize that improving their pricing capabilities requires the understanding and support of every major department and leader in the organization. It is one thing to say that your people should understand their value to customers and that your offerings, sales strategies, and pricing should be defined by this value. It is quite another thing to achieve this goal.

If you try to move too quickly to a value-based approach to pricing, more than likely your efforts will backfire. Customers will rightly be confused and concerned. As a consequence, they will negotiate even harder or, worse, abandon you. Competitors may see your efforts to price differently as an opening to take market share. They'll start undercutting you on deals and put enormous pressure on your sales teams to react. And without the proper training and tools, your sales teams will be defenseless and frustrated by new pricing approaches that don't make any sense to them. Failure to anticipate and manage these forces before they become problems invariably causes pricing initiatives to fail. Your journey will be over before you even get the car out of the driveway.

Rule Nine provides you with some context for the journey to value-based pricing. It starts with a framework to analyze your readiness for the journey and provides some tangible benchmarks by which to monitor your progress.

The Ultimate Objective

Pricing to value is the ultimate objective. The challenge is that many managers underestimate the deep level of cross-organizational change needed to make this approach stick. The results of trying to go too far too fast are sadly predictable. Say somebody gets excited about value and starts an initiative to move to value-based pricing. He succeeds in making changes on a small scale but falters when responsibility for the initiative is necessarily distributed beyond his control. The effort stalls, there are setbacks, and the goal of value-based pricing is discredited. An even worse scenario is when value-based pricing is implemented, but the sales professionals aren't ready for it. They continue to act as if cost-plus pricing were the rule, at the same time giving high-value features or services away, thus undermining the whole effort.

One services firm that we worked with learned all of these lessons firsthand. The company started its pricing journey well. The CEO took the lead in announcing to the world and the investment community that "rational" pricing was a priority and that the firm would be dedicating significant resources to it. The company created pricing departments in each major line of business. It also created a new function that collected and analyzed costing, operations, and competitor pricing data. It put a lot of impressive intellectual effort into creating pricing models that considered value delivered to customers, not just traditional time and materials measures. It soon became clear that the effort was more than the organization could reasonably handle.

Fortunately, the same management team that put this pricing model into place also recognized that it was doing too much, too quickly. With our guidance, the company took some deliberate steps. The first thing they did was assess what was actually possible in some given time frames. From this assessment, they learned what they were doing right and where renewed effort was required. They concluded that their company lacked critical data in such areas as their own costs and competitor pricing. They further concluded that some key systems were not ready to undertake such a large-scale transformation.

In the end, the company kept its long-term vision, but eased up enough to allow the organization time to catch up to the vision. To keep things moving with a focus on more attainable goals, the company developed a pricing maturity model that reflected current and anticipated future capabilities and related them to specific approaches to pricing. That process represented a reasonable set of attainable goals. These were goals that managers could implement and handle on a timely basis.

This progression focused on improvements in three key areas. The first was continued progress on efforts to more tightly define and standardize key service lines so they could innovate to grow. The second was greater data and insight from additional analyses of costs to serve customers so they could price for profits. A third insight was that valuable data could be gathered from failed projects, or projects that did not produce the results the client wanted. These same projects typically exceeded their scope or budget. By analyzing what drove these shortcomings, the firm began to understand the root causes of service failures. This realization allowed the company to improve service value and keep costs under control. This helped the company improve the capabilities of the sales organization to define, measure, and sell value, thus putting backbone in the selling process.

Management determined that it could make all this happen within four years. In the first year, it focused on improving its internal data, making informed assumptions about the value of its services, and getting the right people in place. While it built these critical pieces, the company tweaked its current cost-plus pricing models to reflect its steadily improving knowledge of costs to better leverage their high-value areas. In year two, it set target costs and published detailed pricing guidance for the majority of its offerings. The company even began to increase the use of fixed-price contracts. By years three and four, the company's objectives are to work much more closely with clients to understand value and roll out value-based pricing models for those services where clients could see concrete evidence of value.

Results are very encouraging. By year two of the process, the value of signed contracts increased 32 percent and earnings jumped by $320 million. These impressive results arose from two key insights. The first was that it isn't necessary to achieve some elusive ideal state in pricing in order to see big improvements in financial performance. In fact, that's the beauty of tackling pricing. Small steps forward can produce big results. The second insight was counterintuitive. Successful initiatives to improve pricing are rarely pricing-driven. Our client understood that their vision of improving pricing was going to be enabled by better offering definition, cost management, sales skills, and data. The firm continues to show improvements in revenues and profits. This has been possible because management was honest with itself about what the organization was capable of achieving.

The Two Levels of Pricing

Pricing occurs at two levels: strategic and tactical. The strategic level involves, first, setting pricing and offering strategies and, second, establishing list prices. It is also at the strategic level that firms implement their base pricing approach. They decide if they are going to price to value, use cost-plus pricing, market-driven pricing, or a combination.

At the tactical level of pricing, we manage transaction prices and the rules of engagement for price negotiations. At this level we want to make sure that customers fairly earn discounts and street prices are consistent with long-term strategic objectives. As we discussed in Rule One, if discounting occurs, we want to know that it occurs for a legitimate reason, such as the guarantee of more volume. As shown in Figure 9.1, both strategic and tactical pricing combine the activities that are at the root of pricing with confidence.

Figure 9.1 offers three important insights. First, adjustments at the tactical level can generate incremental revenues (that drop straight to the bottom line) in a relatively short period of time. Second, changes at the strategic level involve processes that can take a long time and a lot of effort to change. Third, change at the tactical level will not last long unless meaningful action is taken at the strategic level. The challenge is how to move forward at both levels by setting

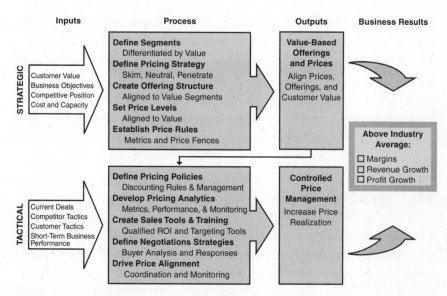

Figure 9.1   The Two Levels of Pricing.

short-term goals that can be reached while continuously moving toward a long-term vision of pricing to value.

What kind of results do these efforts produce? It is well accepted that a 1 percent improvement in price results in an 11 percent boost in net profits. But as we saw in Rule Six, "Add New Products and Services that Give You Negotiating Flexibility and Growth," such a blanket approach leads to an imbalance in prices between those customers that have negotiating power and those that do not. If we go a step further and get tactical pricing processes under control to eliminate unnecessary discounts, we find that typical gains in net profit can exceed 20 percent profit improvement. Finally, if we address both the strategic level *and* the tactical level, improvements well above 20 percent are possible.

Consider the case of a $3 billion semiconductor company that implemented tighter controls on discount management and deal evaluation. To ensure that these controls had impact, they also implemented globally integrated revenue and pricing plans. The firm also invested heavily in new technologies that enabled them to bring innovative new products to market. This combination of tactical discipline and a newly invigorated product line paid handsome dividends. Within 12 months of getting these components rolled out, profits increased by over $400 million. The interesting part of this story is that at the time of this turnaround, this company was still in the very early stages of transforming its pricing capabilities. Let's look at some ways of starting the process.

The Pricing Maturity Model

The key to building a plan to develop your organization's pricing confidence starts with an honest assessment of what your organization is currently capable of achieving. With that understanding, you can select the pricing approach that your organization is most capable of executing in the short run. You can then create a road map that will get you to your long-range goals. Key to this is choosing a pricing approach—cost-plus, market-based, or value-based—that your organization can implement and manage.

Smart pricing leaders know that making changes is a matter of evolution not revolution. They know that they can make significant contributions to profitability, earn credibility, and warm the organization up for further change by showing the financial results of improvements to current pricing approaches. Since most organizations currently employ some form of cost-plus and/or market-based pricing, this is where pricing leaders start. They then adjust the approach and expectations as the organization's pricing capabilities mature. An awareness of this dynamic makes it possible to put together a simple pricing maturity model that benchmarks progress and also points to the best method for choosing how to establish price levels at any point in the evolution. A summary of this model is shown in Figure 9.2.

Most organizations move through a predictable progression, employing successively more sophisticated pricing approaches. Many start with cost-plus pricing. As we saw, cost-plus pricing has

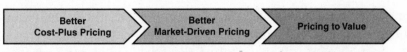

Better Cost-Plus Pricing	Better Market-Driven Pricing	Pricing to Value

• Improve quality of costing data
• Start using incremental costing in pricing decisions
• Use price to control utilization of bottlenecked resources
	• Base prices on:
	  • Qualitative indicators of value
	  • Competitor price levels
	• Adjust cost multipliers based on perceived value
	• Use costs as benchmark for low end of possible price range
		• Must understand offering cost and revenue impacts for the customer
		• And differentiation relative to the competition
		• Take a fair share

Figure 9.2   The Pricing Maturity Model.

advantages and disadvantages. When combined with good managerial judgment, cost-plus pricing can provide good results. The underlying objective is reasonable: Make a profit on everything you sell. An important point about cost-plus pricing is that most organizations are comfortable with it. So on the journey to value-based pricing, it makes sense to start with what many organizations have been using. There is no inherent conflict between cost-plus and value-based pricing. If an organization sharpens the quality of its costing data, it is always in a superior position.

As we saw in Rule Five, "Price to Increase Profits," making the move from setting prices based on average to setting prices based on incremental costing changes everything. It shows quite clearly the impact on revenues and profits of your pricing decisions. Using an incremental costing approach to enable superior pricing decisions is the first step in the pricing maturity process. Applying incremental costing produces what we call *value-enhanced cost-plus pricing*.

The next step in better cost-plus pricing is to start using data on your capacity and bottlenecks to drive decisions on when to raise or lower prices to control utilization of key resources. One pricing manager earned an extra $60 million for her company in a single quarter by applying this concept. She started indexing prices according to available plant capacity. During times of constrained capacity, the pricing manager fully allocated all costs and took a further markup to set prices. During off-peak times, she looked at incremental costs only and added a markup to this lower cost basis. If customers absolutely needed their products during times of peak demand, they paid the highest prices. If they shifted their delivery to off-peak times, their costs and prices were much lower. By better understanding incremental costs, the manager used differential pricing to effectively optimize the utilization of plant capacity.

Once you've achieved confidence in the quality of your costing data, you're ready to move to the next phase: better market-driven pricing. In pursuing better market-driven pricing, organizations must still adhere to the disciplines developed during the first phase of the pricing maturity process. Firms that fail to maintain this discipline while pursuing market-driven pricing quickly find their margins eroding. Such companies simply react to what customers tell them about their prices. The feedback, not surprisingly, is that prices are too high. This is how the cycle of customers playing vendors against each other starts, and every deal becomes heavily negotiated.

Firms that have discipline and a vision of their long-run pricing objectives pursue market-driven pricing much differently. They carefully listen to and analyze what their customers and sales teams are telling them about their value and that of the competition. At first this data may be qualitative. For example, they may go to accounts where they have very high market share and investigate why these accounts choose to give them so much of their business. Usually what they find out is that some of their offerings are far superior to the competition in ways that the customer believes are valuable. At this stage neither the firm nor the customer may know enough to pin down that value, but the knowledge that your customers think you provide greater value than your competitors is enough to successfully implement better market-driven pricing.

This qualitative value data when combined with good costing data enables you to start making adjustments to your cost multipliers when calculating pricing. Let's say that your standard markup is 30 percent. When you start to consider your value and competitive position, you will see that some of your offerings are stronger and others are weaker.

It is a simple process to put this all together. Score each of your offerings in two ways. First, grade each offering on how much value it creates for customers. A three-point scale is appropriate:

3 = High value
2 = Moderate value
1 = Low value

Next, grade each offering on its level of differentiation from the competition. Again a three-point scale is all that's needed:

3 = Differentiated
2 = On par with the competition
1 = Weaker than the competition

With this information in hand, you now have the basis to start adjusting your cost multipliers. For offerings that provide high value and are differentiated, increase the multiplier. Maybe instead of your standard 30 percent markup, you bump it up to 35 percent. Now, compare that result against your strongest competitor to determine if your customers will accept the new prices. For offerings that are in the middle of the pack, change your multipliers so that your prices are consistent with your principal competitors. If your offerings are not differentiated, it's hard to get a premium for them. Finally, for weaker offerings, determine whether lowering prices for them is going to build market share.

This is the type of process that Parker Hannifin used to drive dramatic increases in net income. Parker Hannifin is the world's largest manufacturer of motion control technologies systems. It recently upgraded its pricing model. Parker abandoned its old cost-based pricing model. What did Parker replace it with? Another model that is also cost-based. But Parker Hannifin adjusted its pricing formulas based on the incremental value of the products based on their degree of commoditization. "A" products are pure commodity. "D" products are all specialized or otherwise customized. Products marked "B" and "C" fall somewhere between those extremes, incorporating elements of both commodity and specialization.

Parker Hannifin discovered that it could realize more margin from the "D" products than the "A to C" products. There is nothing surprising about this. Customers are typically more accepting of higher prices as the level of specialization or customization increases. The difficulty, when you have 20,000 products, is distinguishing them in terms of differentiated margin opportunity. Parker Hannifin improved net income by over 500 percent and return on net income by 300 percent. There's more to this story, but we'll save that for Rule Ten, "Price with Confidence: Remember Who You Are."

What's the next step for firms like Parker Hannifin? We predict it will be making the move from qualitative to quantitative measures of customer value. As we mentioned in Rule Two. "Understand Your Value to Your Customer," developing data on customer value is often just a matter of asking your customers the right questions. The real challenge is putting the insights gleaned from that data to work. This involves linking pricing and value in a way that is credible with customers and your own sales team. Sales professionals require the right tools, training, and skills to successfully sell with value-based pricing. This final step in the evolution is a big one. Let's get into some more detail on getting the organization ready.

Criteria for a Confidence-Building Pricing Process

Key to building pricing confidence is the knowledge that what you have planned for and built is going to stand up in the field with sales and customers. Improving your tactical pricing rules and processes is an important element of that building process. Even if you don't have a formal pricing department in place, you can boost revenues just by tightening up your discounting. That is why many firms start their pricing transformation journey here. Given the returns and the fact that getting control of transaction pricing is an effort that is typically led by the pricing function, we need to spend some time detailing the opportunities you can find by improving transaction pricing.

You can walk into just about any company and find plenty of managers who are unhappy with price management. Common complaints include too much discounting; a lack of consistency in how discounts are awarded; and slow, unresponsive price quotations processes. The challenge is that given this litany of pain points, they don't have good criteria for a new process that will set them on the right path. Without agreement on what a good price management process should look like, there is no way to make the pain go away.

A Coherent Pricing Strategy

Any strategy that underpins an effective price management process must perform well in five dimensions: repeatability, visibility, scalability, accountability, and standardization. See Figure 9.3.

Each of these five dimensions is critical to a price management process that has integrity and is easy to understand. Let's look at how each element gets you to this goal.

Repeatability

To what extent do similar customers that buy similar volumes get similar prices? And when they don't, can your organization truthfully and clearly explain the differences? A process is said to be reliable if it produces consistent results. If you provide similar inputs

Critical Objectives	Principal Attributes
Repeatability	Same Input = Same Output
Visibility	Communicated and well understood across entire organization
Scalability	Supports growth and staff transitions
Accountability	Decisions made and data generated at key points in the process are accessible and easily audited
Standardization	80% of pricing covered in standard process, 20% exceptions

Figure 9.3   Criteria to Ensure an Effective Price Management Process.

(customer and deal attributes), a coherent pricing system should generate similar outputs (price). When pricing systems are perceived to be unreliable or unfair, customers tend to negotiate harder. They quickly figure out that if they repeat their demands for a discount often enough, eventually they're going to get one. This system betrays any confidence an organization has in its pricing. Good pricing systems provide the same price for similar customers regardless of how hard they negotiate.

Visibility

When your sales professionals present pricing options to a customer, they need to be able to stand behind what they are saying. To do this, salespeople need to understand how the prices were arrived at. What process was used? What criteria were used to evaluate pricing options? Why are the options being presented to the best customers? Without compelling answers to these questions, the sales professionals will be put on the defensive—and hard-grinding customers will sense weakness.

Many pricing organizations are worried about sharing too much information with the field. They fear that this information will be used to rationalize discounts to customers that don't deserve them. In environments where there are conflicting incentives relating to price, senior executives who are in the habit of overriding the pricing team, and/or low levels of trust, these fears are justified.

Having said that, one of the worst things that a pricing team can do is take a defensive position and make the pricing process seem like a big mystery. This only undermines confidence in pricing. How do pricing managers balance the issues of visibility and abuse of the pricing process? Organizations need to start with a set of realistic objectives. A firm that has a history of antagonism between sales and marketing and conflicting goals and incentives is not going to be able to move to a well-controlled and visible pricing process overnight. Such organizations need to crawl before they walk and walk before they run.

We suggest picking a few achievable goals at first. Examples include closing the gap between list and realized prices by a defined amount over a defined period of time, instituting price floors, or eliminating some unnecessary giveaways such as extended payment terms or overly generous return policies. These are good starting points because they are consistent with the objective of visibility. For each, it is easy to envision a business case for making the change and a simple set of rules for how the business case will be achieved. These small wins become mutual confidence-building measures. They show how sales, marketing, finance, and pricing can all come together to do something that every responsible manager wants to do: make more money. As these diverse groups learn that they can work together on mutually acceptable pricing goals, the benefits of the pricing process become clearer.

Scalability

As pricing processes mature beyond confidence-building quick wins, priorities inevitably shift to scalability. In the past, many pricing transformation efforts have been wrecked on the shoals of scalability. Systems that were run by particularly astute managers and/or were managed using simple software like Microsoft Excel often failed when the scope of the job increased. Managers can ask a few simple questions to determine if they are ready to scale the pricing process. The foundation argument that must be made: Do we have a set of pricing policies that are (1) consistent with business objectives and (2) reflect the realities of interacting with our customers? Other important questions to ask along the way are as follows.

Process
- Are the major steps of the price management process defined?
- Do our policies and process work in support of each other?
- What percentage of transactions are covered by the process?
- Is there a defined process for identifying, approving, and managing exceptions to pricing policy?

People
- For each step of the pricing process, are there clear owners?
- Do these process owners have the information that they need to be successful?
- Do the process owners have the necessary skills?
- Does the organization have a means for identifying and training critical players in the pricing process?
- Do the critical players have the genuine and unwavering support of senior management?

Technology
- Have we identified the key pieces of analysis that need to be performed at each step of the pricing process?
- Do our information systems provide the data needed to perform the required analysis?
- Have we sufficiently addressed all prior questions so that we can benefit from the use of price management software?

Accountability

One of the most interesting aspects of a strong pricing process is the window that it provides on the day-to-day activities within the business. With the right people, processes, and technology, firms can drill down to the level of individual transactions to understand the impact of customer, competitor, and managerial actions, one sale at a time. To get to this level of insight, firms need well-defined data and analytics for each step of the process. In addition, work flows and approvals must be defined and documented. When these factors come together, you have a process that enables managers to measure results and determine accountability for those results.

Consider the story of one executive who called us about a $20 million deal that he wanted to sign with a major customer in the European market. The executive wanted to close the deal because this was a marquee account, and he felt that it would add a boost to the sagging image of his company's brand. The problem was that the customer was seeking a low price, a very low price. We helped the executive review the impact of the proposed deal on existing contracts with other customers. This analysis showed that the $20 million deal would be more than offset by $60 million in lost revenues. The loss would arise from price protection clauses in existing contracts and from demands for lower prices from customers that found out about the deal. We recommended against it.

Nevertheless, the executive took the deal and the accountability that went with it. By being associated with the customer's prestige, the brand became more popular and became the centerpiece of a turnaround of the entire business. Both revenues and market share doubled, swinging from an operating loss to yearly operating income of over $600 million. The gamble paid off. The executive made the decision based on a reasonably complete set of data and analysis. He also saw something in the deal that the numbers didn't show, and that's something you can't learn in business school. Our main point is that the manager was prepared to be accountable for his decision. In this case it worked out, and he received a big bonus and promotion.

Standardization

Once organizations start down the path of pricing process transformation, there is one simple measure that can reveal how ingrained the process is. Each organization should set objectives for the percentage of deals that flow through the standard pricing process and the percentage that are treated as exceptions. This one measure provides significant insight into two key areas: relevance of the process and organizational adoption.

To make an impact, any major business process must be viewed as relevant to current business conditions. If a process isn't used for the *majority* of the cases that it is designed to handle, the system is at risk. If a firm develops and rolls out a new pricing process and only 20 percent of all deals are controlled by the process, what message does it send to the field and to customers? It actually sends several messages, and none of them are good:

- You might get a better price by working outside of the process.
- Using the process is likely to be an impediment to quickly getting useful answers to customers' pricing questions.
- Senior management is timid and/or not serious about making real changes to the way that pricing is handled.

Add up these messages and they say, "Wait a few months, and it will be back to business as usual."

Final Thoughts

The key to improving your pricing confidence is to pick a path that your organization can follow. Rare is the organization that can quickly make the move to value-based pricing. Even if they are capable, their customers and competitors will often not be very accommodating. Start with the low-hanging fruit. There is a lot of money to be made simply by improving your discounting controls. Start there and build up to become better at setting prices and defining your pricing approach. The full evolution may take years. But at each step, you are sharpening your organization's sense of its value to its customers and driving improvements in results that will make your company more profitable, more competitive, and more confident.

RULE TEN

Price with Confidence:
Remember Who You Are

Customers buy results, not rhetoric. Moving beyond the rhetoric of value will enable you to prove those results to customers. By applying these 10 actionable rules, you can have confidence in your pricing decisions. You can move the negotiation to a discussion of how you provide concrete results for your customers. Your firm will earn more profits and revenue by capturing the money you're currently leaving on the table.

Who owns value? The ultimate answer, of course, is "everyone." More specifically, you do. Everyone in the value chain—everyone who designs, produces, or consumes the product or services—owns a piece of the resulting value. But in order to make pricing with confidence a reality in your company, processes must be put in place to integrate the goals of individuals, departments, and the organization as a whole into a cohesive go-to-market plan, offering by offering. We argue that without a sustained focus on developing a systematized value process by a senior leader in the firm, talking about pricing with confidence is meaningless rhetoric that quickly becomes a program of the month, ignored at the end of the quarter when a company needs to meet its sales goals.

Let's take a look at the rest of the story we started in Rule Nine.

Parker Hannifin's CEO Donald Washkewicz took on the pricing beast and, as we told you, improved net income by over 500 percent and return on net income by 300 percent based on his improved cost-plus pricing strategy.

What was Washkewicz's real secret to success? It was actually quite simple, yet disciplined. As the CEO, he took the time and made the effort to acknowledge that at least on some of its products, Parker Hannifin provided value it could capture. As a result, the company aligned its pricing with that recognized value. Washkewicz developed the tools to say, "Wait a minute" to hungry salespeople and their customers who were clamoring for lower prices. He had the confidence to act on the basis of Parker Hannifin's self-professed mission statement: to be a supplier of high-value products and services. Washkewicz used that knowledge to price with confidence. His people followed and so did the results.

Simple vision, yes, but, the devil as always is in the details. The biggest problem was convincing Parker Hannifin managers and sales professionals that they would actually benefit from the new pricing mantra. In the words of one executive, the company had to "reprogram the company's management DNA."[1] The president or CEO is the best person in the company to force those changes because changes like these need a champion at the very top. Salespeople and their managers must know with absolute certainty that there is a place where the buck stops.

Does Parker Hannifin still have farther to go in its pricing evolution? Of course it does. Washkewicz will be the first to admit that this game has no ending. It continues as competitors and customers create new playing fields. Like all companies, Parker Hannifin has to continually do a better job of understanding the actual value of shorter delivery cycles and special product features. It also has to get the sales force to believe in the value of the products, as well as the integrity of the pricing process.

An important goal for all companies is to identify where and how certain products and services are better than those of their competitors. Then someone has to lead the charge in recognizing that value, quantifying it, and putting it into a competitive context. Based on that information, salespeople can start to feel good about what they are selling. This way when a customer says there is no value, the salespeople remember who they are, what company they work for, and they begin to price with confidence and support that value.

Support the Value Leader

Senior leadership has the challenging assignment of making sure that everyone in the organization keeps their focus on improving and better leveraging value for customers. To support the value leader, the president or CEO should understand the interconnectivity of departmental activities and implement metrics that track to optimal results for the integrated organization rather than a silo approach. The CEO and/or president should make certain that the approach and process of rollout by the leader involves everyone in the company. When senior managers have a value focus, they can start to manage systems within the organization using effective controls that begin to look at overall quality of output in production and customer retention. Sales managers can help salespeople focus on bringing in *profitable* business rather than *any* business. New goals can evaluate how marketing managers improve the effectiveness of salespeople and how that turns into increased margin and profit for the firm.

Kudos to Accenture, and its CEO, William Green, for focusing on how consultants can share risk with clients while adding to the bottom line results of their clients. And those results are impressive. Accenture increased the number of employees by 25 percent in the past year, a time when many professional services firms are still struggling to use the people they have.

Over 30 percent of Accenture's contracts include some type of performance measures, and more are expected to include these types of provisions in the future. Financial measures include internal cost cutting and improved customer satisfaction. By focusing on client results, Accenture has been able to provide clients with measures of value which help justify fees and create follow-on work—the lifeblood of professional services firms. They price with confidence.

There are a number of short-term steps that can start the customer value process and add revenue and profits fairly quickly to the company. Start by asking senior sales and marketing vice presidents how their people create value with their activities. Follow up with even more specific questions:

- How do you segment the market so that salespeople can focus on high-value prospects?
- What does marketing do to make the jobs of salespeople easier?
- Do you have a clear understanding of how your products and services perform relative to the competition?
- Do you know how that performance difference converts to financial benefits for customers?

How do you make sure that your salespeople have information about your competitors and use it effectively in their dealings with customers? By answering the following questions:

- What can you do with your offering, positioning, and negotiating skills to improve closing rates without using price as the primary lever?
- Are the right salespeople focused on the right accounts?
- Are sales reps trained and motivated to focus on transactions with price buyers only or do they have the skills to drive value with relationship customers?

A Process of Discovery

These questions should start a process of discovery in your company that moves the activities in the direction of customer value. It should also begin to build the foundation that will limit price-only negotiations, which are so devastating to profits. The important point is that to accomplish that end, companies need to align customer segmentation. They need a clear process of offering development and sales efforts to provide customers with what they value, making sure they pay a fair price for it. Everyone in the organization needs to hold on to the reality that they really do provide value to customers, and that it's their obligation to leverage that value with fair pricing.

To move the company to the direction of customer value, it is necessary to actually visit customers. We tell our clients that pricing professionals should conduct at least 10 customer visits each month. Does this sound excessive? Look at exceptional business leaders like Jack Welch (General Electric), Herb Kelleher (Southwest Airlines), and John Chambers (Cisco Systems). Each of these leaders is a fanatic about spending time in the field with customers. Using these visits to ask questions about the customers' business is the most powerful tool the senior executive has. Not only does it tell the customer that they are important to the relationship, it connects the executive in the most direct way with what is going on with the customer in a competitive environment. Customers will also tell you what they need from you in a real sense. When managers act on these insights, they create real opportunities for differentiation and long-term competitive advantage.

It's important that the customer meeting be about the customer's issues. Unless the customer brings up questions about sales or service, we counsel our clients to leave the company's sales or support issues and/or agendas back at the company. Request in-person meetings with a variety of customers to gain the best understanding of how your products and services impact the customer's business in bottom line dollar results. Ask what you are doing well and what you can be doing even better. Ask for ways to improve and then listen. This is not the time for defensiveness. Ask for the painful anecdotes. The customer surely has some. Let the customer know that its candor you want. Managers who stay highly connected with customers have a much clearer vision of what needs to be done in the firm.

Follow up internally to ensure feedback is given to product management and that, where possible, findings are implemented by

operations. Give the sales teams a chance to see the customer feedback and company responses. Compare management response with
customer input to determine if they are sticking to their senior-level
commitments.

Next, organize executive teams to develop strategies that have
direct connections with how product marketing and salespeople pursue various customer segments and with how resources are allocated.
The essence of good strategy is the allocation of the resources where
they have the best result. Don't spend the resources unless you have
a good understanding of what the alternatives are and how each
will increase profits. This will provoke clear and universal agreement
on the segment structure for customers and the relative value that
each segment represents. Then the price discounts and/or marketing
funds will be used in segments and with customers that will yield the
highest returns.

Ask managers to identify the market sweet spots, such as ones
where customers are dissatisfied with the competition and ready to
change. Develop concise strategies to identify (1) target markets
that make sense for the company, (2) products that have value for
that target, and (3) selling approaches that use value as the basis
for negotiation rather than price. One benefit of this approach is
that the companies begin to understand which customers are not
worth the resources they consume. As the CEO of one of our clients
says, "The juice ain't worth the squeeze." Therefore, this exercise
should not be done on customers with high volumes and low price;
it should be done on those who could reward you with better profit.

The other aspect of this exercise is to insist on relentless data
collection of current discounting practices. The first cut of data can
be collected and put into an Excel spreadsheet to provide you with
some terrific and compelling insights. While you're at it, take a look
at competitive activities, wins and/or losses, pricing, competitive
performance in market segments, product differences, and new features. Begin to develop systems of measurement and control around
the fundamentals of value. Metrics should include competitive market share statistics, growth in market share, profit, and revenue by

segments. Review, realign, and set simple metrics for the activities required in each department to deliver value to customers. Salespeople, dealers, and partners should be aligned to perform complementary activities. Their opportunities should be based on how they perform on these activities. Should sales volume be part of it? Sure. Just remember that sales incentives on volume alone fail to capture *all* of the right activities, especially value trade-offs during negotiations rather than price discounts.

The HR department can develop training programs for employees on the value-based approach and pricing with confidence. Be clear about each person's role, responsibilities, and performance criteria. Inspect what you expect. Test-run the training yourself, to ensure it is simple and basic, so that action items and take-aways are effectively implemented. Successful companies have performance systems that encourage people to attend the training and reward them as well. Further, include posttraining tools and follow up to make sure that people are putting the training to work in meaningful and profitable ways.

Insist on aggressive but fair timelines that people can meet. Every day that companies delay putting in a value-based program is the equivalent of ripping up dollar bills (one of our favorite motivational visuals). Have the patience to let people learn as they go, but insist on accountability toward a measurable process with clear and time-based action steps. Challenge the steps and the timing. People like to be safe, especially in changing environments. It is up to managers to ask more of people and push them outside their comfort zone. A sense of urgency starts at the top and ends in the ranks of employees.

Don't settle for abstract answers to rhetorical questions. Ask for specific data in each area. If managers don't have it, implement a process to start collecting and reporting on useful information. Require managers to identify how their primary activities and those of their subordinates assist in the value creation or capture activities of the company. If they have an initiative that requires approval, make sure resulting value is part of the process. And, follow up and inspect that the value is delivered when the project is completed.

This kind of training demonstrates that all employees live up to the company's value proposition.

It all comes together when each element of the departmental goals is tested and aligned with a companywide, integrated go-to-market plan focused on the customer. The result is an understanding of how each element of the integrated organization participates in its value activities. Leaders need to look at the activities of people and tools in an economic process rather than as a series of isolated silos. For example, consider a manager who is making a decision to purchase a new piece of equipment for her operation. One question she may want to answer before making the decision might be: If higher-quality products can be produced by this equipment, will customers pay for the higher quality? Questions like this will help people understand how they participate in the value process, learn what is expected in decision processes, encourage interdepartmental collaboration, and eliminate many of the unrelated approaches we see today.

If companies focus on the value exchange with customers, they will identify opportunities to create better value for customers with their offerings while moving away from a commodity orientation. Another result is that products and services within the portfolio are bundled to take advantage of differing levels of value. Then the company can offer choices with a range of high- to low-value bundles to meet the differing value needs and buying behaviors of customers.

Sales' Role in Customer Value

Salespeople need to have a high and low offering so they have trade-offs to use when negotiating with customers. It's the best and sometimes only way to bluff the poker players. A low-value offering doesn't have to be as profitable as others because its primary purpose is to protect the prices of high-value offerings. It's a negotiating tool that is used instead of price to close a deal. It is also a way for customers to better understand and discriminate between different solutions.

We remember one senior manager, a vice president of sales, who had just learned this technique. Regrettably, his company hadn't had time to roll out flanking products. This manager found himself in the middle of a tough negotiation with a division of General Motors. Car manufacturers have the reputation for being some of the toughest poker players in business. When GM's purchasing agent demanded a lower price for a critical component, the sales manager responded, "No problem, we already have a cost-reduced version of this product. Here is the catalog number." After a conversation about the differences between the lower- and higher-cost products, the purchasing agent concluded that the lower-cost product would cause problems in the exhaust system that could eventually lead to a product recall. He didn't want to risk that, so the purchasing agent approved the use of the higher-priced product. That one tactic not only closed the order but it also bluffed a very difficult purchasing agent and dropped close to a million dollars to the bottom line of the business.

Provide salespeople with tangible value messaging and ROI calculations to show customers how much financial benefit they accrue from the use of your company's products or services. A value approach makes sure the salespeople are compensated and well managed so they secure more profitable business, rather than *any* business. And with their tools and training, they emerge victorious from difficult customer negotiations. Finally, prices established based on customer value should be rolled out to salespeople, dealers, and partners with high levels of discipline and control. Don't let salespeople or senior managers avoid the training. Ensure they understand that their job is to have confidence in pricing and the value of that confidence. If they don't, your job is to give them that confidence. Period.

The net result is more pricing power and less negotiating with customers. When customers are served with high-, medium-, and low-value product choices, both revenue *and* profits increase. We saw one company employ this high-, medium-, and low-value product approach several years ago. The senior leadership team was highly involved with the initiative. When it was rolled out with a training program to the field sales force, the president of the company introduced very aggressive sales and profit objectives for the year. The following year, after talking about the results with the VP of sales who led the effort, he advised us that not only had they exceeded their sales objectives by a wide margin, but they had *doubled* their profit from pricing improvements over objectives for the year—an increase of over $6 million.

Your results can be equally dramatic. But even if they are not, when managers take control of their markets, their customers, and their organizations in a consistent and thoughtful manner they drive confidence. Managers who shore up their people with more confidence in price and make it part of their daily mantra dramatically increase the sales and profits for their company.

Why Most Companies Fail

The 10 rules in this book have all advised you to create more valuable customers. We don't expect this to be an easy process. This is because organizations are made up of people who are driven to perform activities the way they have done so in the past. But markets continually change. Competitive advantage is more elusive than ever. In order to implement customer value recommendations and see the benefits of revenue and profit growth, you and your company are going to need to change. We recently met with the CEO of a hi-tech company we helped a number of years ago. During the meeting he said, "I've always wondered why your stuff never had any traction here." The answer was simple. First, there was only one person on his senior staff, our sponsor, who believed in this approach and implemented it with his sales force. The marketing and product managers were involved, but the rest of the senior leadership did not invest in adoption. When our sponsor left the company, no one carried the process forward.

Early on, the company used our process to close their biggest and most profitable customer. They had to negotiate with a tough poker-playing purchasing agent. The salespeople believed in the price because they knew it was based on much higher value than the competitor's solution. They loved getting some pricing power when they negotiated with tough customers. They successfully closed a $100 million piece of business that took over $13 million off the table and put it in their company's pocket.

Successful managers are willing to bet on the long-term impact of customer value to make companies successful. Consider Boeing. Its management has repeatedly made huge investments in new aircraft and technologies to make the company better and more competitive. Has Boeing come close to the brink? Sure. But each time, the investment starts to pay off. Like a lumbering, overweight jetliner trying to take off on a long runway, individual products may take a long time to take off. But investors know that when Boeing does gain some altitude, it will soar. Boeing did it with the 737, the 747, the 777, and now the 787 Dreamliner.

Go on a Value Hunt

A number of years ago, we learned a very effective leadership technique. It's called a *lion hunt*. It is a way to find out what is really going on in your firm, what is bothering people, and what they are really worried about. In some ways it is an offshoot of the principle of Managing by Walking Around (MBWA) described in *In Search of Excellence* by Tom Peters and Robert Waterman.[2] But it is different from MBWA in that a lion hunt requires managers to actually sit down with people in the bowels of the organization. It is an unstructured, open-ended discussion where the manager does a little probing and spends a lot of time listening. It was a great way to stay connected with the problems of the firm and make sure we were dealing with the right issues.

We suggest a variant of this exercise we call a *value hunt*. Talk to your production people, your service people, your salespeople, and your customers. Yes, we did talk about this in Rule Six, "Innovate for Growth," but that concerned people outside the organization. Now we want you to extend your discussion to people inside your company, as well. Ask them what they think your company does well, and what they think your company does poorly. Ask them why they think that. Ask them a question we often ask in a customer engagement: How do you feel about the company? Simple questions lead to complex answers.

Your people are down in the trenches. They deal with and know about the real problems of the company. Managers, especially senior managers, are often isolated from those problems. They are wearing rose-colored glasses. They believe their own rhetoric about how great the firm is. Confidence in pricing means moving beyond the rhetoric. It means removing the rose-colored glasses and getting real about what your company does for your customers. Good leaders understand the problems, fix them, and get their people to move beyond the problems and gain some real confidence in the value of the things their firm does for its customers.

One of our leadership heroes is Anne M. Mulcahy of Xerox. Bill George writes about her story in his book *True North*.[3] The book describes how Anne Mulcahy took over a company that was on the brink of failure. Confidence was in short supply at Xerox. The company was out of cash and its once mighty reputation for technical innovation was tarnished. Mulcahy was suddenly responsible for 96,000 Xerox employees around the world. What saved the company was Mulcahy's willingness to discover the truth and act on it. She asked Xerox people hard questions and listened to the even harder answers. And she talked to customers, lots of them. Once she stabilized the firm, a Herculean task, she insisted all of the senior executives go out and talk to customers. During the process, the managers learned what Xerox was doing well and what it wasn't doing well for customers. One of Anne Mulcahy's mantras is to turn every employee into a customer-facing builder of value. Every executive, even staff vice presidents such as the head of human resources or accounting, owns specific customer relationships. These are the go-to people whenever there are issues of customer satisfaction with Xerox products. The Xerox team developed priorities for fixing the problems and earned the trust of their customers.

Confidence in Value Breeds Confidence in Pricing

Todd Bradley came into HP's PC division at the request of new CEO Mark Hurd. He found a struggling division that was losing market share to Dell and other brands. Other PC manufacturers were desperate to beat Dell, but in so doing they played right into Dell's hands. Bradley was determined to make Dell respond to HP. In two years, Bradley changed HP's game plan and regained revenue, share, and profitability in the once-declining division.

Former HP CEO Carly Fiorina and her executive team had tried to attack Dell where it was strongest—in direct retail sales with low prices. That didn't work. Bradley did something we like to recommend—go with your strength. He saw that HP's strength was in distribution. Bradley went on a value hunt. He visited hundreds of distributors and dealers. He listened to their concerns, fixed their problems, earned their confidence, and made distribution once again a key element of HP's strategy. His timing was perfect as PC shoppers are moving in droves to laptops and want to see those laptops before they buy them, something Dell's model cannot provide. Where Fiorina had invested in big, general brand image advertising, Bradley shifted advertising dollars to the point of customer contact—at the retailer. In doing so, he sent a strong message to the dealers that HP was once again supporting their efforts. Is he letting Dell control the direct channel? Not exactly. He is also quietly improving their direct service levels and has seen share rise almost 25 percent, taking most of it out of Dell. Confidence in value breeds confidence in price.

If employees have a low opinion of the company, how do you expect them to have confidence in pricing? This is not some gushy rhetoric; this is real. If you want people to have confidence in pricing, they've got to have confidence in the company. If you want them to have confidence in the company, they've got to have confidence in the leadership. That sometimes takes bold moves. We saw HP regain its confidence.

Consider the story of the man who said "No" to Wal-Mart. Everyone thinks that saying "No" to Wal-Mart's insatiable demands for pricing concessions is business suicide. But with a firm conviction of the value you offer and confidence in your pricing, it's possible to negotiate with the toughest customers and survive. This is true, even if it means losing a large piece of business. Sometimes you've got to let that big customer go if they are undermining the confidence in your value and pricing.

Jim Wier was the CEO of Simplicity, the parent company of Snapper, the popular lawn mower maker. At one time, Wal-Mart represented 20 percent of Snapper's sales. But then Wal-Mart insisted that Snapper reduce its prices even further. The world's largest retailer dangled the promise of dramatically more volume. If Snapper did not discount its prices, Wal-Mart would move to one of Snapper's competitors.

Most CEOs faced with this challenge would have swallowed hard and accepted the take-it-or-leave-it offer for which the mass retailer is so feared. But Wier understood the Snapper brand and that its promise of quality, durability, and innovation could not be sustained in the face of such price reductions. Wier had confidence in the value the Snapper brand created for customers. He had confidence in the strength of his dealer network. He had confidence in his prices and knew that he needed to set a standard for that confidence. Wier said good-bye to Wal-Mart and chose to lose a fifth of his business overnight. He did so because Snapper had four things going for it. First, Wier understood that Snapper's brand had value in the marketplace. Two, he had evidence that customers were willing to pay for that value. Three, he had confidence that his remaining dealer organization would grow the business. Four, he had confidence in Snapper's pricing.

Snapper redoubled its commitment to sell its line of lawn mowers through a network of 10,000 independent dealers who understood the product and could service it if something went wrong. This level of service was something Wal-Mart could not provide. In addition, dissolving Snapper's relationship with Wal-Mart made the dealers happy (no one wants to compete with Wal-Mart). It took pressure off the dealers' margins and allowed them to stock more Snapper inventory. Within the first year, Snapper got back most of the business it lost to Wal-Mart by winning back the hearts of the dealers. Now that's what we call confidence in pricing.

We're not saying that any of this is easy. It takes commitment, coordination, and discipline of multiple activities and individuals. It takes changes in systems and processes. It takes a willingness to take a chance. Selling conditions in BTB markets are tougher than ever with more competitors, low-cost players, faster cycles to commodization, mergers, private equity buy-outs, just to name a few. Successful companies move beyond the rhetoric of value to tangible provable value. Make it real for your people and your customers, and you will increase their confidence in your prices.

Notes

1. Timothy Aeppel, "Seeking to Perfect Prices, CEO Tears Up the Rules," *Wall Street Journal*, March 27, 2007.
2. Tom Peters and Robert Waterman (1982). *In Search of Excellence: Lessons from America's Best-Run Companies*, New York: HarperCollins.
3. Bill George (2007). *True North: Discover Your Authentic Leadership*, New York: Jossey-Bass.

INDEX